BY ALEJANDRO GALMARINI

Keyboard Chords

Made Easy

Learn to Play, Read, and Write Chords in **Standard Chord Notation**

VISUAL SYSTEM

Includes 480 illustrations
of positions in all keys

Galmarini, Alejandro
   Keyboard Chords Made Easy / Alejandro Galmarini. - 1a ed. -
Olivos : Jorge Alejandro Izuel, 2023.
   52 p. ; 29 x 21 cm.

   ISBN 978-987-88-9131-6

   1. Música. I. Título.
   CDD 780.71

Galmarini, Alejandro
   Keyboard Chords Made Easy / Alejandro Galmarini. - 1a ed. -
Olivos : Jorge Alejandro Izuel, 2023.
   Libro digital, PDF

   Archivo Digital: descarga y online
   ISBN 978-987-88-9132-3

   1. Música. I. Título.
   CDD 780.71

Dedicated to Raúl Julio Izuel

ISBN 978-987-88-9131-6
ISBN 978-987-88-9132-3

PROLOGUE

When I ask my musician colleagues to tell me about the first step in their musical careers, they often tell me stories about getting their first instrument or album, or when they first heard a particular artist that moved them.

In my own case, I'm surprised I can't remember how it all started. What I do remember vividly from my musical beginnings is a feeling that still burns in me with the same intensity as back then. It is an insatiable curiosity of wanting to discover how music works, a deep desire to know the "trick" behind what I hear and see every time I come across music in any of its manifestations.

How can it be that while one person plays a melody on a violin and a pianist plays something different, together it all sounds marvelous to our ears? How does a pianist know what to do to accompany the acrobatics of a human voice? How can a pianist or guitar player interpret a melody and also accompany it with many other notes? And how do they know which notes to use? Or, if a guitar player and a pianist get together and want to play, but they don't have a score, how do they know what to play? Why do some notes sound so good together, and others don't? Why do certain notes together communicate a sense of calm, while others communicate tension? And later, when it comes to creating, how do I accompany a melody? What sounds can I use in a song? And, of course, how can I communicate a feeling or message by combining sounds?

With time and study, I've found a lot of these answers through access to knowledge of musical harmony, which explains how sounds are related to each other and what happens when two or more sounds occur simultaneously. Knowing what chords are and how they're built is essential. This knowledge will give us strong tools to speak the same language with other musicians and be able to read and write songs in a universal language. Above all, it will allow us to gain mastery of sounds and use them to communicate and share the music that lives inside us.

The aim of this book is to concisely and clearly, but also completely, share all the tools you'll need to gain mastery of how chords are created and written in the Standard Chord Notation system.

Quickly, visually, and without having to sit through long courses on musical language, you'll be able to put your fingers on the keyboard and bring sounds to your ears, without having to take on all the complexities of staff notation.

I'll show you all the mechanisms you'll need to read, write and play any kind of chord, whether you want to compose, accompany a song, or just broaden your musical knowledge.

I'm sure you're going to enjoy it.

Alejandro Galmarini

TABLE OF CONTENTS

STANDARD CHORD NOTATION

Throughout this book, we'll learn a system called *Standard Chord Notation*. This is probably the most widely used system nowadays because it gives us a simple way of writing and reading musical notes and chords, allowing us to communicate and achieve understanding among musicians. In this book, you'll learn to gain mastery of it, which will allow you access to a huge quantity of music.

MUSICAL NOTES

Musical sounds are represented as musical notes. There are 7 of them, and you'll find them written in *solfège* or *American notation*. In American notation, each note corresponds to a capital letter:

Solfège	Do	Re	Mi	Fa	Sol	La	Si
American Notation	C	D	E	F	G	A	B

NOTES ON THE KEYBOARD

To correctly locate notes on the keyboard, it's very important to pay attention to its design. You'll see that the black keys are grouped in alternating sets of 2 and 3. The note **Do (C)** is located under and to the left of the first black key in each group of 2.

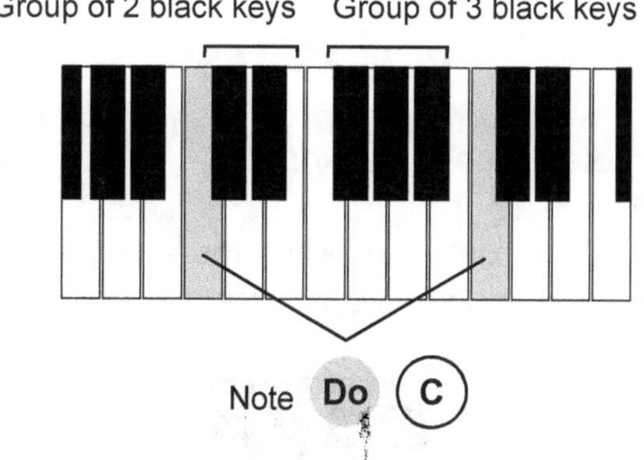

From **Do (C)**, we can easily find the rest of the notes because they coincide with the white keys. You'll see that this design is repeated several times along the keyboard, which means that the notes keep repeating.

This group of 7 notes with its black keys is called an octave. Pianos traditionally have 7 octaves and 4 more notes (88 keys), but different instruments with keyboards have a varying quantity of octaves.

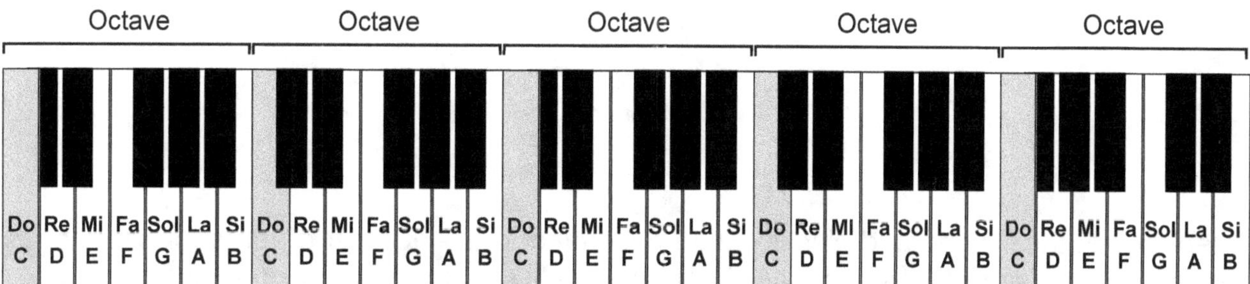

ACCIDENTALS

While there are 7 notes located on the white keys, we can also find intermediate sounds located on the black keys of the keyboard to alter the existing notes.

When we alter notes by raising them (towards the right of the keyboard), we use the sharp symbol (♯), and when we alter them by lowering them (towards the left of the keyboard), we use the flat symbol (♭).

Notes that don't have a black key above them (**E** and **B**) can also be raised, and the ones that don't have a black key below them (**F** and **C**) can be lowered.

You'll find that the same key or note can receive different names depending on which note we have in mind when we name it. For example, the first black key can be called **Do sharp** (**C♯**) or **Re flat** (**D♭**). This is called an enharmonic note.

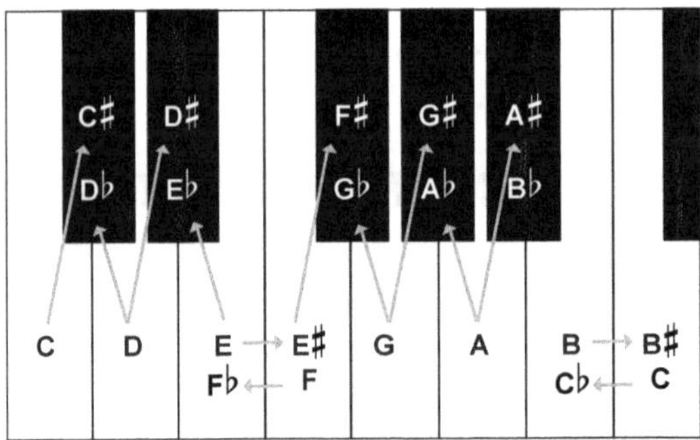

INTERVALS

The distance between two notes is called an *interval*.

The minimum distance that can exist—two keys that are next to each other—is called a *semi-tone* (½ tone). Two consecutive semi-tones form a *tone*.

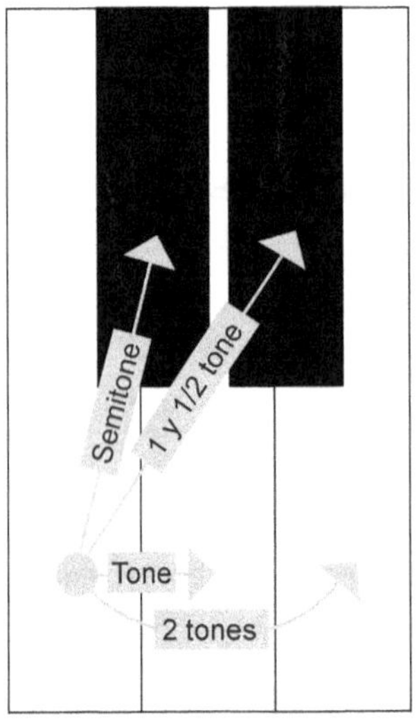

Intervals get their name and classification according to the number of tones or semi-tones that separate their notes. In the following table, you'll see the existing intervals.

Number of semi-tones	Number of tones	Interval (Classification)	Nomenclature	
0 semi-tones (two notes making the same sound)	0	Unison	1	Simple Intervals
1 semi-tone	1/2 tone	Minor Second	♭2	
2 semi-tones	1 tone	Major Second	2	
3 semi-tones	1 y 1/2 tone	Minor Third	♭3	
4 semi-tones	2 tones	Major Third	3	
5 semi-tones	2 y 1/2 tones	Perfect Fourth	4	
6 semi-tones	3 tones	Augmented Fourth or Diminished Fifth	#4 / ♭5	
7 semi-tones	3 y 1/2 tones	Perfect Fifth	5	
8 semi-tones	4 tones	Augmented Fifth or Diminished Sixth	#5 / ♭6	
9 semi-tones	4 y 1/2 tones	Sixth or Diminished Seventh	6 / ♭♭7	
10 semi-tones	5 tones	Minor Seventh	♭7	
11 semi-tones	5 y 1/2 tones	Major Seventh	7	
12 semi-tones	6 tones	Octave	8	Compound Intervals
13 semi-tones	6 y 1/2 tones	Minor Ninth (Minor Second)	♭9	
14 semi-tones	7 tones	Ninth (Major Second)	9	
15 semi-tones	7 y 1/2 tones	Minor Tenth (Minor Third)(Augmented Ninth)	#9 / ♭10	
16 semi-tones	8 tones	Major Tenth (Major Third)	10	
17 semi-tones	8 y 1/2 tones	Eleventh (Perfect Fourth)	11	
18 semi-tones	9 tones	Augmented Eleventh (Augmented Fourth)	#11	
19 semi-tones	9 y 1/2 tones	Twelfth (Perfect Fifth)	12	
20 semi-tones	10 tones	Minor Thirteenth (Diminished Sixth)	♭13	
21 semi-tones	10 y 1/2 tones	Thirteenth (Sixth)	13	

When the distance is more than an octave, the intervals are called compound. It's useful to associate compound intervals with the corresponding simple interval since it's really the same note, one octave higher.

For example: the minor ninth (♭9) is the same note as the minor second (♭2), the ninth is the same note as the major second (2), etc.

Intervals in relation to Do (C)

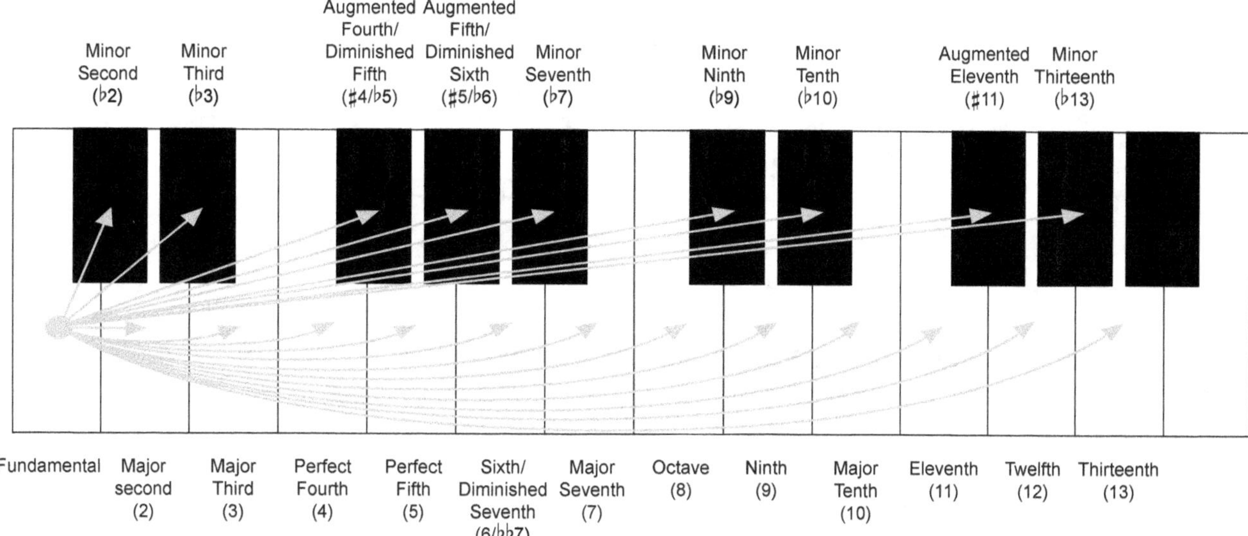

Creative tip

You can understand intervals beyond their mathematical aspect, that is, counting the tones and semi-tones they contain. Here are some things you can do to learn to recognize them by sound and by getting your fingers used to their position and distance:

• Practice playing each interval in ascending order, first the lower note and then the higher one.

• Play them in descending order, first the higher note and then the lower one.

• Play both notes at the same time.

• Practice forming and playing each interval from each of the twelve notes.

CHORDS

When two or more musical sounds are played at the same time, a chord is created.

There are many types of chords, according to the number of notes they contain and the types of intervals that exist between them or, in other words, the distance that separates each of the notes that are being played simultaneously. The same type of chord can be created from any of the 12 notes.

In general, when we use chords to accompany melodies, as is the case with most songs, we can say that each chord is a selection of notes made by the musician in order to accompany the melody in a particular fragment of the song.

We can simplify this graphically as follows:

Now we'll take a look at the relationships that exist between the notes of each type of chord and start to create and practice them.

TRIADS

This is the most common type of chord and is the starting point for all the other types of chords. It gets its name from the fact that it's made up of three notes.

The four basic triads are created by separating their three notes by intervals of a third. Because there are two classes of intervals of a third, the minor third and the major third, we get four possible combinations.

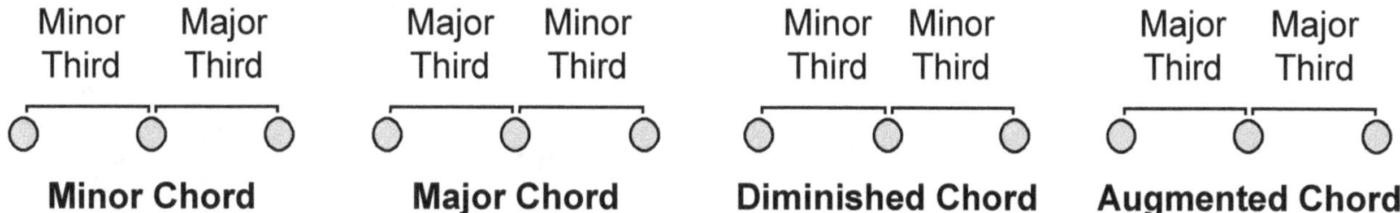

CHORDS INTERVALS FORMULA

The set of intervals that determine each type of chord is called the chord interval formula, and it's written by indicating the names of the intervals we should use based on the first note, or root, used to form that chord.

Let's take the example of the minor chord made by superposing a *minor third* and then a *major third*. Its interval formula will be **1 - ♭3 – 5** because it's made up of the root (**1**), the minor third (**♭3**), and the fifth (**5**). This interval is formed between the root and the third note, which we get by adding a major third on top of the second note.

If we apply this formula beginning with any note we choose as the root, we will be building the **minor chord** of that note.

For example:
If we apply it beginning with the note **Do (C)**, the chord will be **C minor**.
If we apply it beginning with the note **Re (D)**, the chord will be **D minor**. These are the resulting notes:

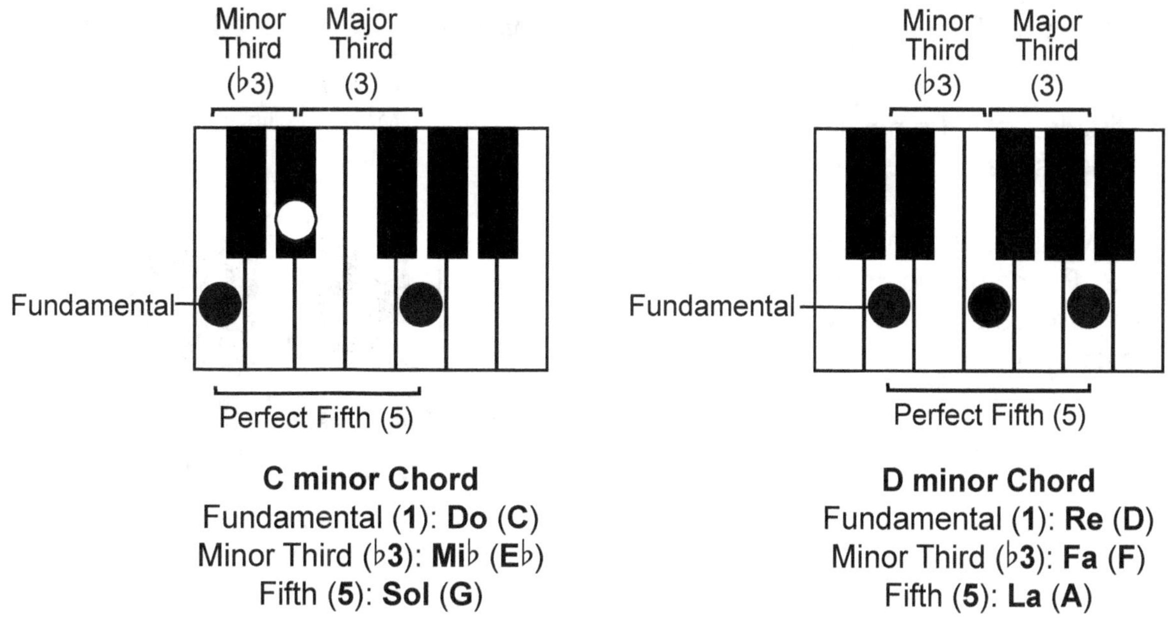

C minor Chord
Fundamental (**1**): Do (C)
Minor Third (**♭3**): **Mi♭ (E♭)**
Fifth (**5**): **Sol (G)**

D minor Chord
Fundamental (**1**): **Re (D)**
Minor Third (**♭3**): **Fa (F)**
Fifth (**5**): **La (A)**

The following types of chords will be built using the note **Do** as an example, but their interval formula will work like a "recipe" to build this type of chord starting with any note.

MINOR CHORD

As we have seen, this type of chord is made by superposing a *minor third* (1 and ½ tones) followed by a *major third* (2 tones). This last note is a perfect fifth in relation to the root (3 and ½ tones).

Notation	Chord name	Interval formula
Cm	**C minor**	**1 - ♭3 - 5**

- The first letter of the notation (**C**) determines the chord's root note.

- The **m** following the root indicates that it is a minor chord.

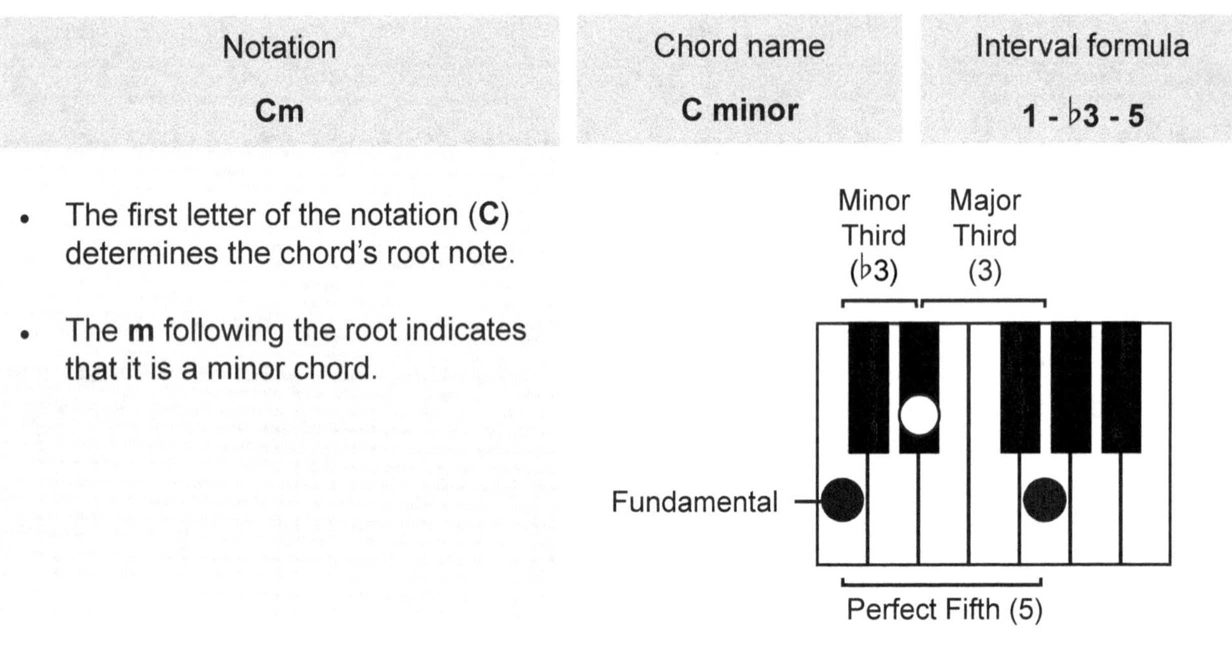

MAJOR CHORD

This type of chord is made by superposing a *major third* and then a *minor third*, forming a perfect fifth in relation to the root.

Notation	Chord name	Interval formula
C	**C major**	**1 - 3 - 5**

- The first letter of the notation (**C**) determines the chord's root note.

- By convention, only the root note is used for major chords, without adding any other symbol to indicate their type.

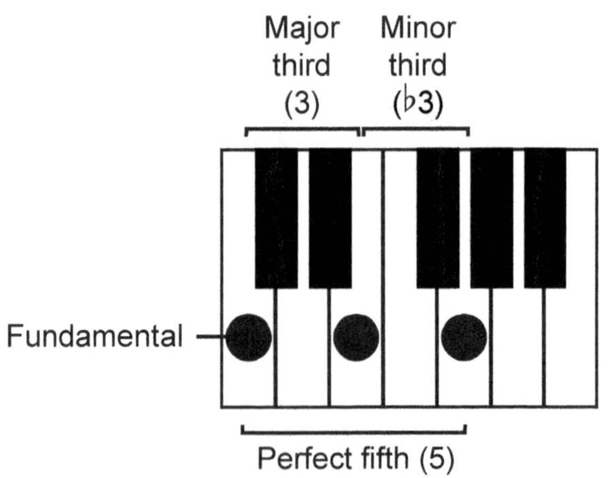

DIMINISHED CHORD

This type of chord is made by superposing two *minor thirds*. The third note is a diminished fifth in relation to the root, and this is where the name of the chord comes from, even if it is a chord in the minor mode.

Notation	Chord name	Interval formula
C°	**C diminished**	**1 - ♭3 - ♭5**

- The first letter of the notation (**C**) determines the chord's root note.

- The ° symbol following the root note indicates that this is a diminished chord and that its fifth is diminished.

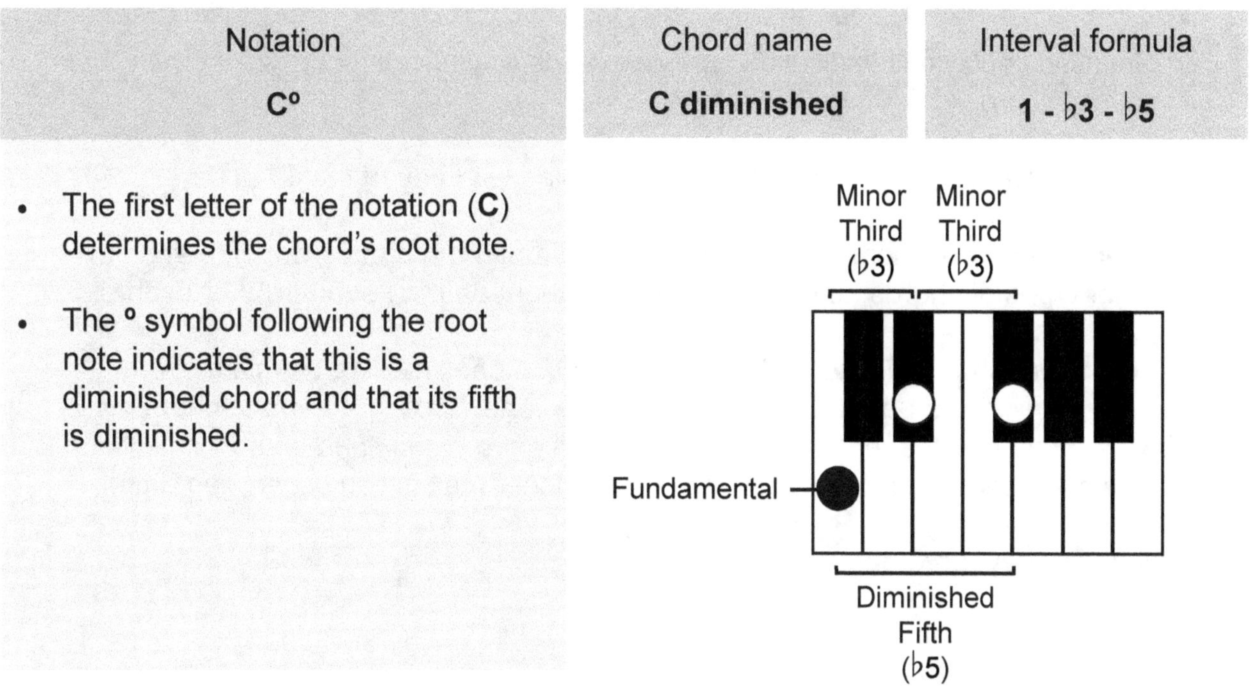

AUGMENTED CHORD

This type of chord is made by superposing two *major thirds*. The third note creates an augmented fifth in relation to the root, and this is where the name of this chord comes from, even if it is a chord in the major mode.

Notation	Chord name	Interval formula
C+	**C augmented**	**1 - 3 - ♯5**

- The first letter of the notation (**C**) determines the chord's root note.

- The + symbol indicates that it is an augmented chord and that its fifth is augmented.

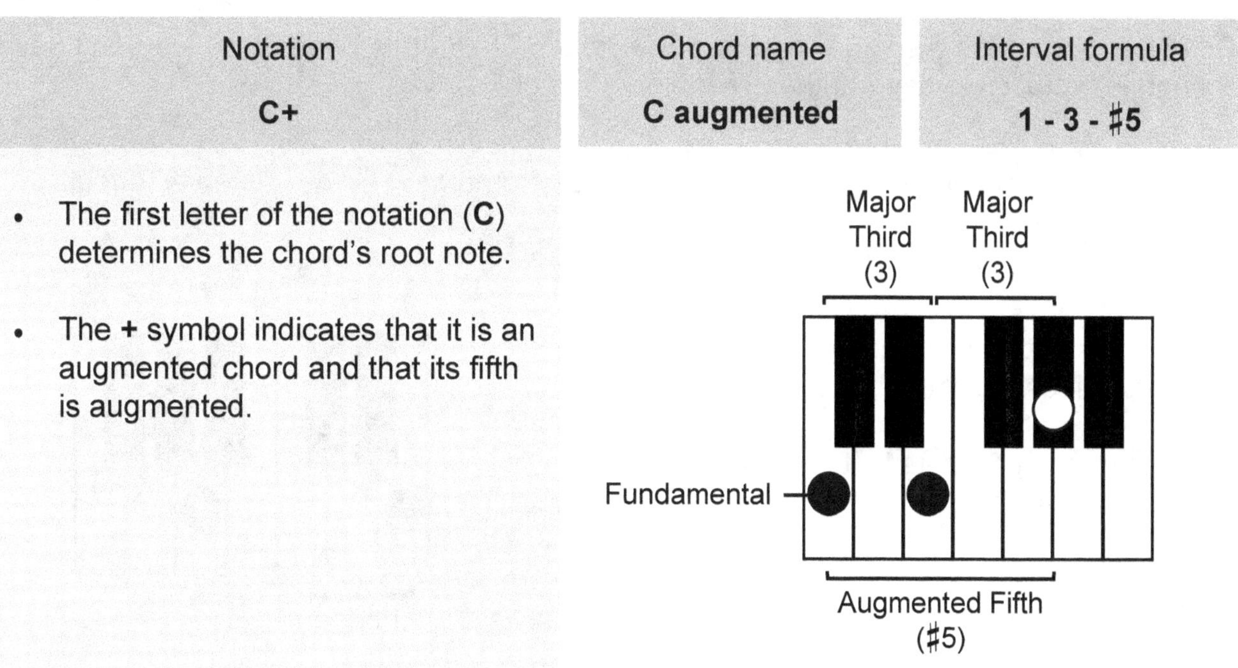

Creative tip

After you understand the interval formulas that make up each chord, I recommend following these suggestions so you can move beyond the theoretical aspect and quickly put this knowledge into practice so it becomes part of your musical DNA.

- Get used to playing the different types of chords so you can recognize them by their sound.

- Practice creating each type of chord beginning with any of the 12 notes.

- Learn to deduce chords not just through their interval formula but in relation to other types of chords, and practice playing them on the keyboard. For example:

Take a *major* chord and diminish its third by half a tone. You'll get a *minor* chord.
Take a *minor* chord and raise its third by half a tone. You'll get a *major* chord.
Take a *minor* chord and diminish its fifth. You'll get a *diminished* chord.
Take a *major* chord and augment its fifth by half a tone. You'll get an *augmented* chord.

Try it on the keyboard!

ALTERED THIRD CHORDS

FIFTH CHORD

This type of chord is also known as a *power chord*. Its *third* is *omitted*, so we don't have enough information to say whether it's major or minor.

Notation	Chord name	Interval formula
C5	**C fifth**	**1 - 5**

- The first letter of the notation (**C**) determines the chord's root note.

- The number **5** refers to its perfect fifth interval.

SUSPENDED SECOND CHORD

The third of this chord is replaced by the second (**2**). It works as a replacement for the third of both a minor and major chords.

Notation	Chord name	Interval formula
Csus2	**C** **suspended second**	**1 - 2 - 5**

- The first letter of the notation (**C**) determines the chord's root note.

- The **sus2** symbol means suspended second.

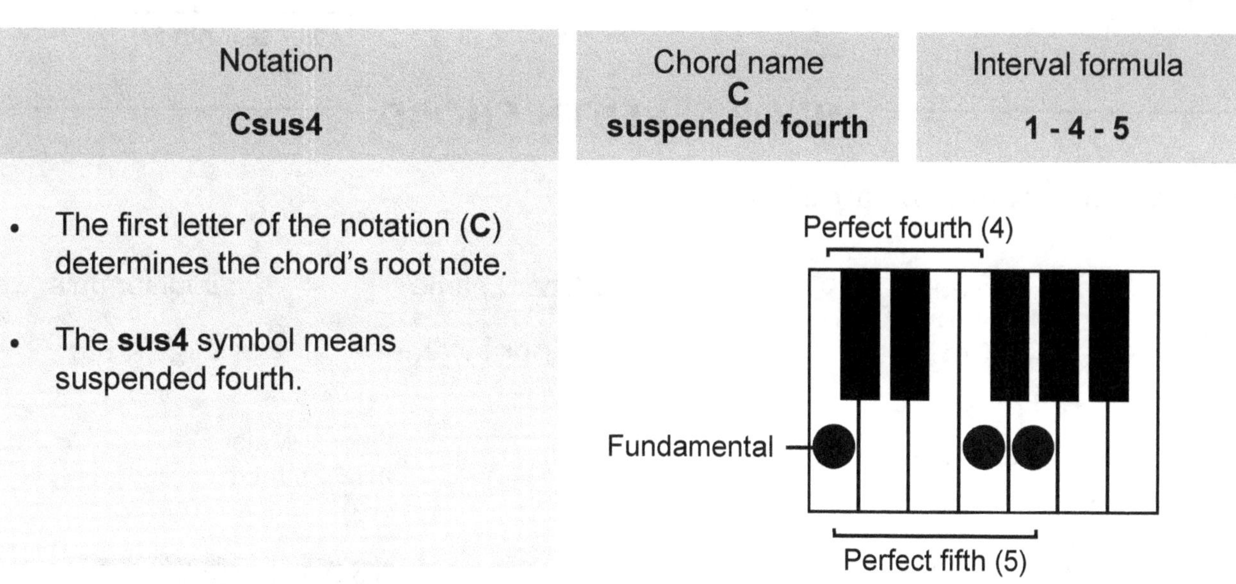

SUSPENDED FOURTH CHORD

The chord's third is replaced by the fourth (**4**). It works as a replacement for the third in both minor and major chords.

Notation	Chord name	Interval formula
Csus4	**C** **suspended fourth**	**1 - 4 - 5**

- The first letter of the notation (**C**) determines the chord's root note.

- The **sus4** symbol means suspended fourth.

SEVENTH CHORDS

We get this type of chord by adding a seventh interval in relation to the root of the triad. For minor, major, and augmented chords, we usually add the minor seventh ($\flat$7) and the major seventh (7). For diminished chords, it's more common to add the diminished seventh ($\flat\flat$7) and the minor seventh ($\flat$7). This gives us the next 8 possible combinations:

———— MINOR MAJOR SEVENTH CHORD ————

We add a major seventh to a minor triad.

Notation	Chord name	Interval formula
Cm(maj7)	**C minor major seventh**	**1 - $\flat$3 - 5 - 7**

- The first letter of the notation (**C**) determines the chord's root note.

- The **m** following the root indicates that it is a minor chord.

- The (**maj7**) symbol indicates that the seventh is major.

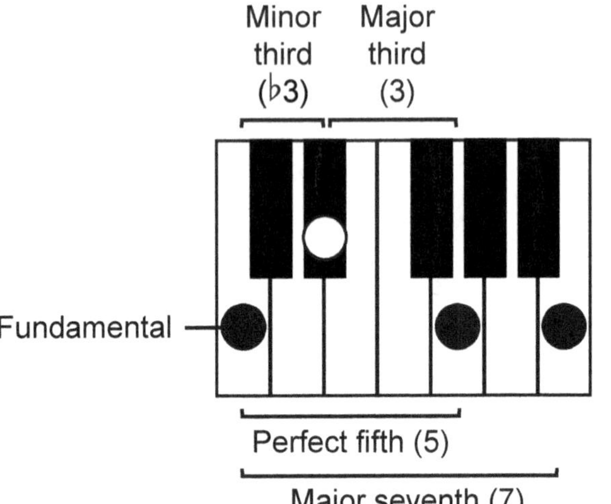

———— MINOR SEVENTH CHORD ————

We add a minor seventh to a minor triad.

Notation	Chord name	Interval formula
Cm7	**C minor seventh**	**1 - $\flat$3 - 5 - $\flat$7**

- The first letter of the notation (**C**) determines the chord's root note.

- The **m** following the root indicates that it is a minor chord.

- The **7**, without any other notation, indicates that the seventh is minor.

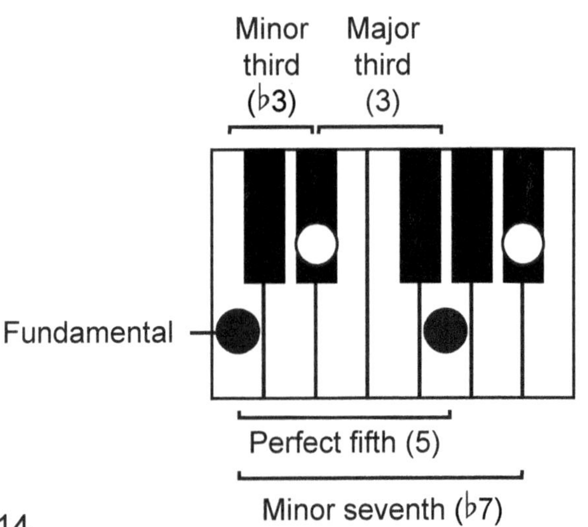

MAJOR SEVENTH CHORD

We add a major seventh to the major triad.

Notation	Chord name	Interval formula
Cmaj7	**C major major seventh**	**1 - 3 - 5 - 7**

- The first letter of the notation (**C**) determines the chord's root note.

- By convention, major chords don't take any symbol to indicate their major third.

- The **maj7** symbol indicates that the seventh is major.

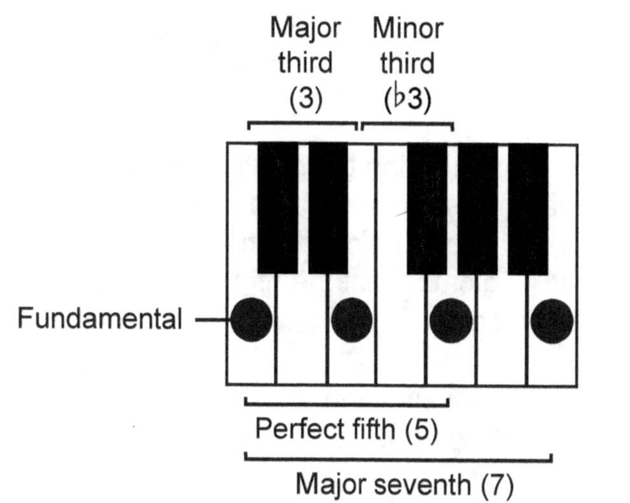

DOMINANT SEVENTH CHORD

We add a minor seventh to the major triad. This is also known as a dominant chord.

Notation	Chord name	Interval formula
C7	**C dominant seventh**	**1 - 3 - 5 - ♭7**

- The first letter of the notation (**C**) determines the chord's root note.

- By convention, major chords only take the letter of their root, without adding another symbol to indicate their type.

- The **7**, without any other notation, indicates that the seventh is minor.

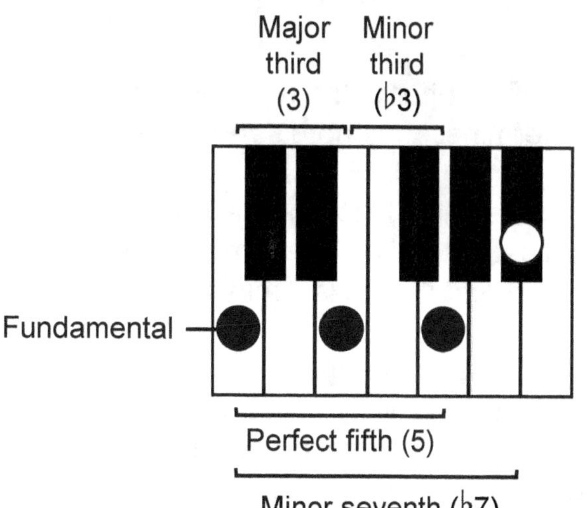

HALF-DIMINISHED SEVENTH CHORD

We add a minor seventh to the diminished triad.

Notation	Chord name	Interval formula
Cm7($\flat$5)	**C half-diminished seventh**	**1 - $\flat$3 - $\flat$5 - $\flat$7**

- The first letter of the notation (**C**) determines the chord's root note.

- The **m** following the root indicates that this is a minor chord, but in this case, the clarification ($\flat$**5**) indicates that the fifth is diminished.

- The **7** indicates that the chord has a minor seventh.

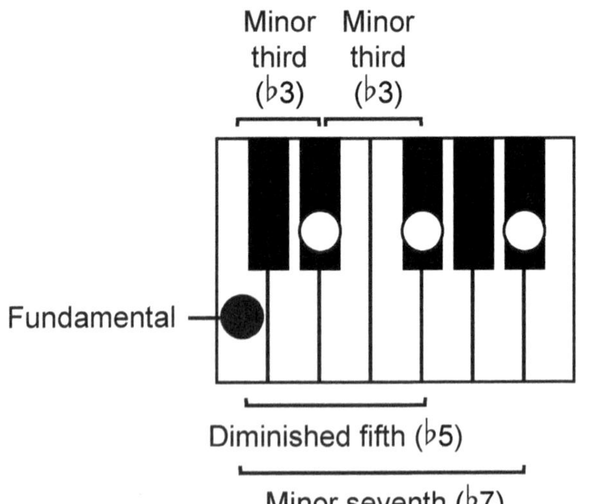

DIMINISHED SEVENTH CHORD

We add a diminished seventh to the diminished triad.

Notation	Chord name	Interval formula
C°7	**C diminished seventh**	**1 - $\flat$3 - $\flat$5 - $\flat\flat$7**

- The first letter of the notation (**C**) determines the chord's root note.

- The **°** symbol following the root indicates that this is a diminished chord and its fifth is diminished.

- In this type of chord, the **7** indicates that it has a seventh, in this case a diminished seventh. By convention, the notation is simplified so that the diminished symbol is not repeated for the fifth and the seventh.

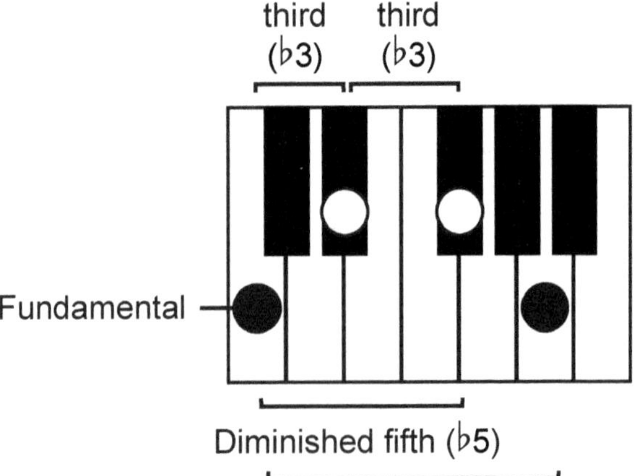

We add a major seventh to the augmented triad.

Notation	Chord name	Interval formula
Cmaj7(♯5)	**C augmented major seventh**	1 - 3 - ♯5 - 7

- The first letter of the notation (**C**) determines the chord's root note.

- The chord's extension is notated like a major chord with a major seventh (**maj7**) whose fifth has been augmented (**♯5**).

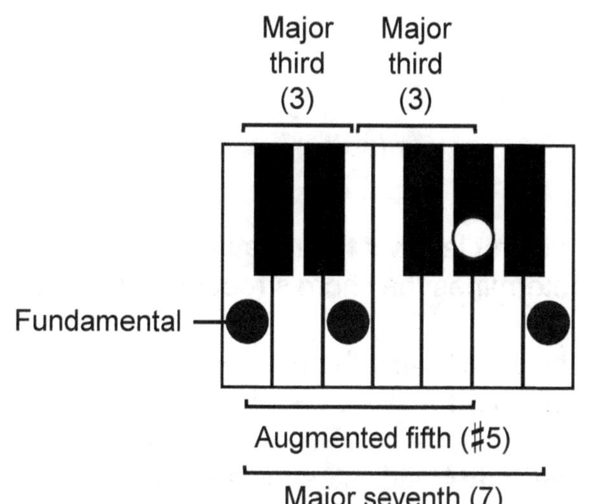

──────── **AUGMENTED SEVENTH CHORD** ────────

We add a minor seventh to the augmented triad.

Notation	Chord name	Interval formula
C+7	**C augmented seventh**	1 - 3 - ♯5 - ♭7

- The first letter of the notation (**C**) determines the chord's root note.

- The **+** symbol following the root indicates that it is an augmented chord and its fifth is augmented.

- The **7** indicates that this chord has a minor seventh.

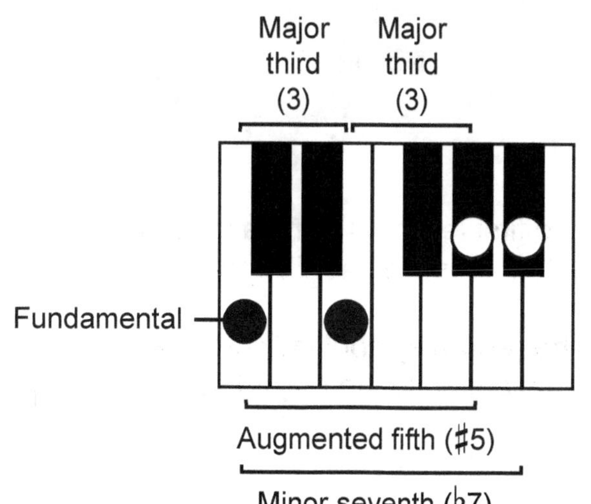

TRIADS WITH EXTENSIONS

An extension is a note that is added to the basic structure of the chord (root, third, fifth, and seventh).

MINOR ADDED-FOURTH CHORD

We add a fourth to the minor triad.

Notation	Chord name **C minor add fourth**	Interval formula
Cm(add4)		**1 - ♭3 - 4 - 5**

- The first letter of the notation (**C**) determines the chord's root note.

- The **m** following the root indicates that this is a minor chord.

- The (**add4**) indicates the added fourth. In the case of minor chords, this is written in parentheses.

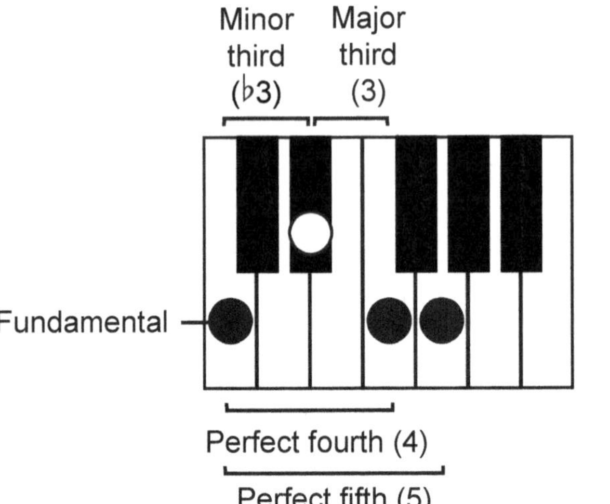

ADDED-NINTH CHORD

We add a ninth to the major triad. We can also use the second, which is the corresponding simple interval. Since it's the same note, it fulfills the same harmonic role.

Notation	Chord name **C major add ninth**	Interval formula
Cadd9		**1 - 3 - 5 - 9**

- The first letter of the notation (**C**) determines the chord's root note.

- The (**add9**) symbol indicates the ninth added to the major triad.

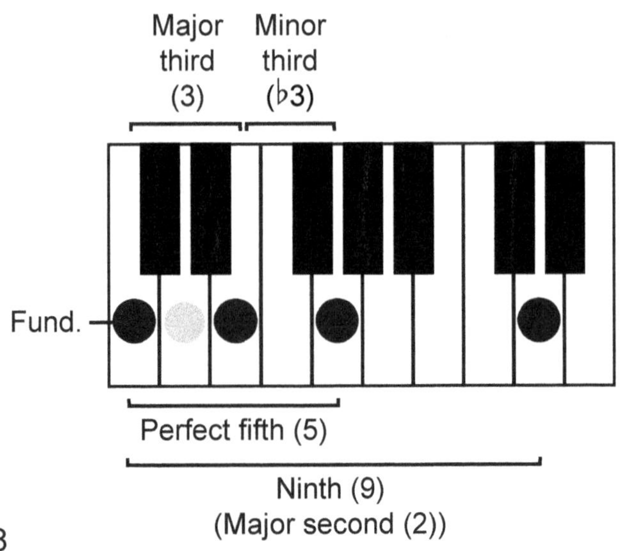

MINOR ADDED-NINTH CHORD

We add a ninth to the minor triad. We can also use the second, which is the corresponding simple interval. Since it's the same note, it fulfills the same harmonic role.

Notation	Chord name	Interval formula
Cm(add9)	**C minor add ninth**	**1 - ♭3 - 5 - 9**

- The first letter of the notation (**C**) determines the chord's root note.

- The **m** following the root indicates that this is a minor chord.

- The (**add9**) symbol indicates the added fourth. In the case of minor chords, this is written in parentheses.

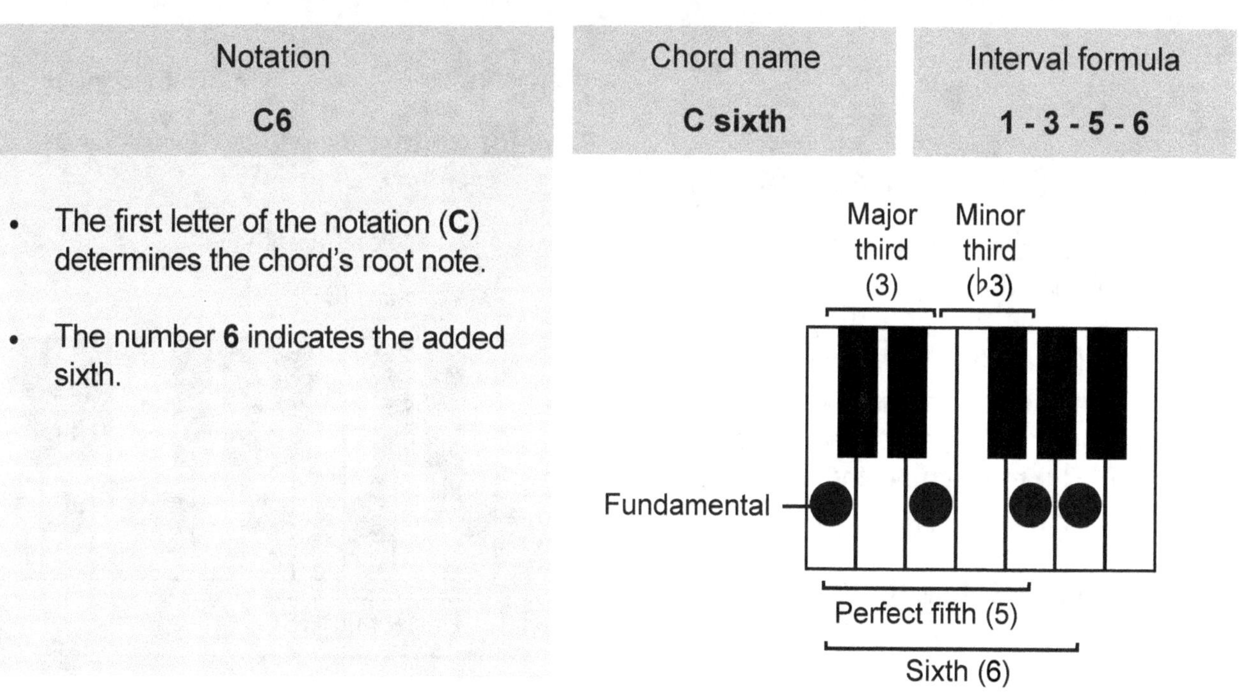

MAJOR SIXTH CHORD

We add a sixth to the major triad.

Notation	Chord name	Interval formula
C6	**C sixth**	**1 - 3 - 5 - 6**

- The first letter of the notation (**C**) determines the chord's root note.

- The number **6** indicates the added sixth.

We add a sixth to the minor chord.

Notation	Chord name	Interval formula
Cm6	**C minor sixth**	**1 - ♭3 - 5 - 6**

- The first letter of the notation (**C**) determines the chord's root note.

- The **m** following the root indicates that this is a minor chord.

- The number **6** indicates the added sixth.

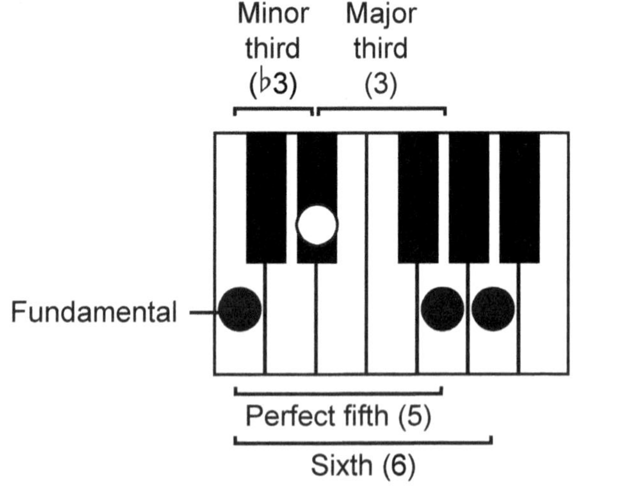

SEVENTH CHORDS WITH EXTENSIONS

MAJOR NINTH CHORD

We add the major seventh and ninth (compound second) to the triad. The result is a maj7 chord with a ninth.

Notation	Chord name	Interval formula
Cmaj9	**C major ninth**	**1 - 3 - 5 - 7 - 9**

- The first letter of the notation (**C**) determines the chord's root note.

- When the ninth is not added, the use of the seventh is implied, so the notation is simplified by leaving out the 7. The **maj** symbol indicates that the seventh is major.

- The number **9** indicates the ninth.

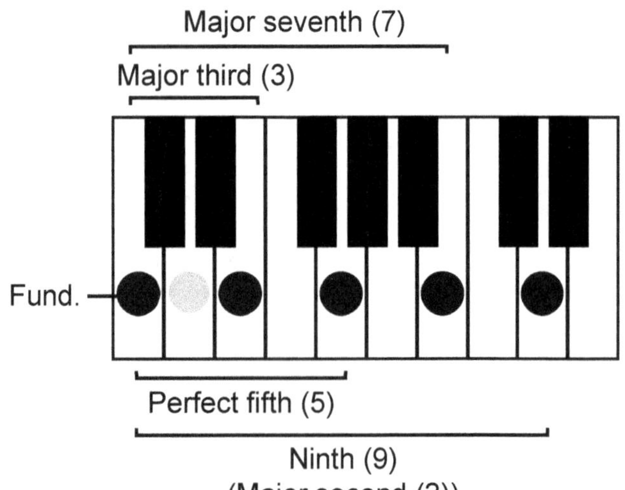

DOMINANT NINTH CHORD

We add a minor seventh and ninth to the major triad.

Notation	Chord name	Interval formula
C9	**C dominant ninth**	**1 - 3 - 5 - ♭7 - 9**

- The first letter of the notation (**C**) determines the chord's root note.

- When the ninth is not added, the seventh is implied. The notation is simplified by leaving out the 7 that corresponds to the minor seventh and differentiating from the major ninth chord with a major seventh (Cmaj9).

- The number 9 indicates the ninth.

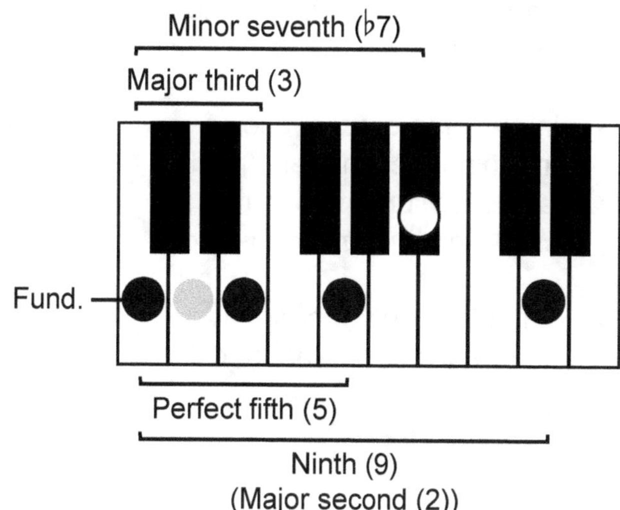

MINOR NINTH CHORD

We add a minor seventh and ninth to the minor triad. It can also be seen as a minor chord with a minor seventh and ninth.

Notation	Chord name	Interval formula
Cm9	**C minor ninth**	**1 - ♭3 - 5 - ♭7 - 9**

- The first letter of the notation (**C**) determines the chord's root note.

- The **m** following the root indicates that it is a minor chord.

- When the ninth is not added, the seventh is implied. The notation is simplified by leaving out the 7 that corresponds to the minor seventh.

- The number **9** indicates the ninth.

DOMINANT ELEVENTH CHORD

We add an eleventh to a major chord with a minor seventh and ninth.

Notation	Chord name	Interval formula
C11	**C eleventh**	**1 - (3) - 5 - ♭7 - 9 - 11**

- The first letter of the notation (**C**) determines the chord's root note.

- In eleventh chords, use of the minor seventh and ninth is implied, but the notation is simplified by leaving them out.

- (3) In this kind of chord, we usually leave out the third.

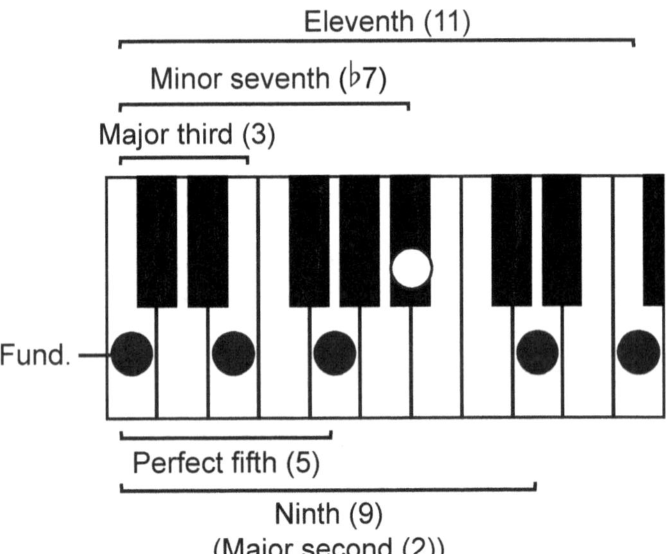

MINOR ELEVENTH CHORD

We add an eleventh to a major chord with a minor seventh and ninth.

Notation	Chord name	Interval formula
Cm11	**C minor eleventh**	**1 - ♭3 - 5 - ♭7 - 9 - 11**

- The first letter of the notation (**C**) determines the chord's root note.

- The **m** following the root indicates that it is a minor chord.

- In eleventh chords, use of the minor seventh and ninth is implied, but the notation is simplified by leaving them out.

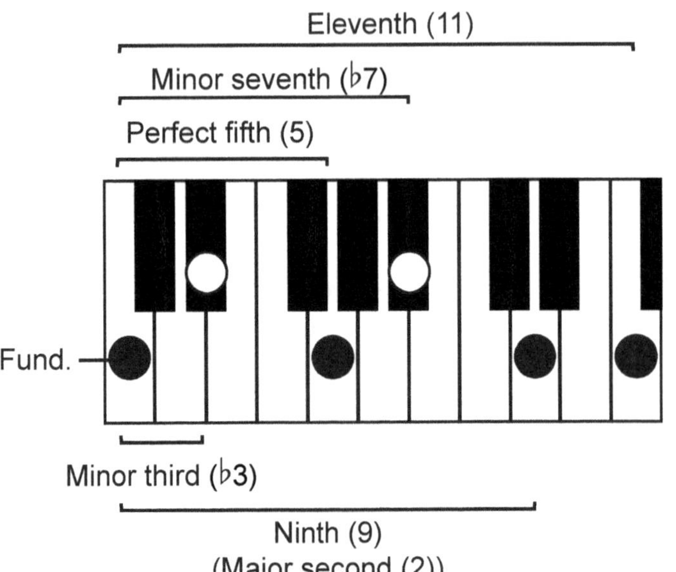

We add a ninth, eleventh, and thirteenth to a major chord with a minor seventh.

Notation	Chord name	Interval formula
C13	**C dominant thirteenth**	**1 - 3 - 5 - ♭7 - 9 - 11 - 13**

- The first letter of the notation (**C**) determines the chord's root note.

- In thirteenth chords, use of the minor seventh, ninth, and eleventh is implied, but the notation is simplified by leaving them out.

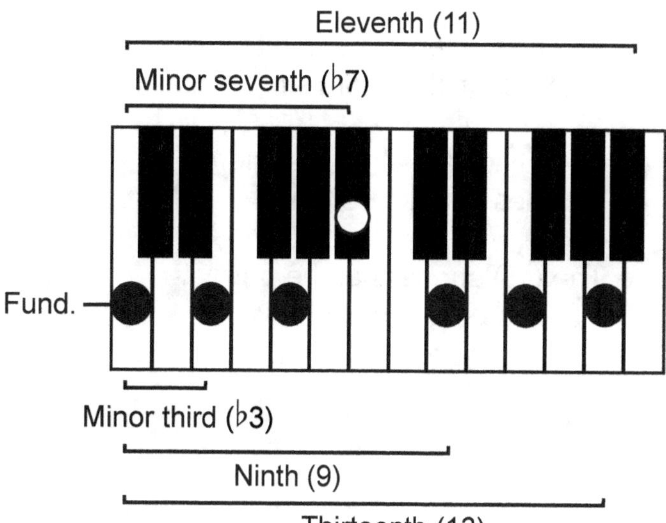

SEVENTH SUSPENDED FOUR CHORD

This is a major chord with a minor seventh where we replace the third with the fourth.

Notation	Chord name	Interval formula
C7sus4	**C seventh suspended fourth**	**1 - 4 - 5 - ♭7**

- The first letter of the notation (**C**) determines the chord's root note.

- The **7** indicates that the chord includes a minor seventh.

- The **sus4** symbol shows that the third has been replaced by the fourth.

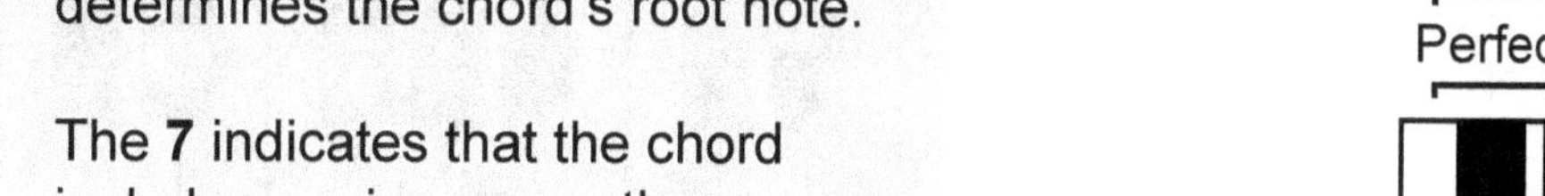
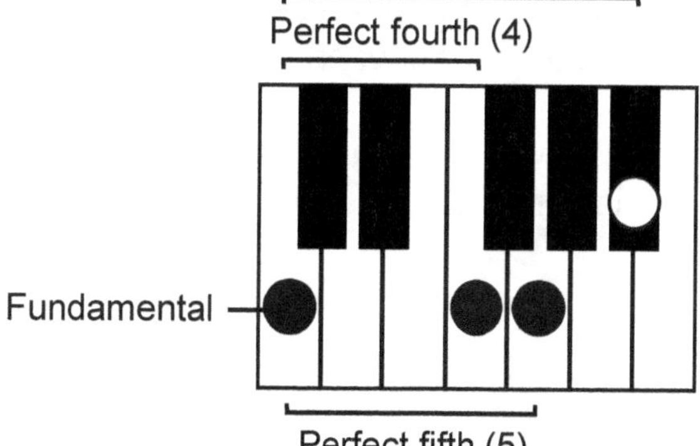

This is a major chord with a minor seventh (Dominant chord) where we replace the perfect fifth with a diminished fifth.

Notation	Chord name	Interval formula
C7($\flat$5)	**C dominant seventh flat five**	**1 - 3 - $\flat$5 - $\flat$7**

- The first letter of the notation (**C**) determines the chord's root note.

- The **7** indicates that the chord includes a minor seventh.

- The ($\flat$**5**) shows that the perfect fifth has been diminished.

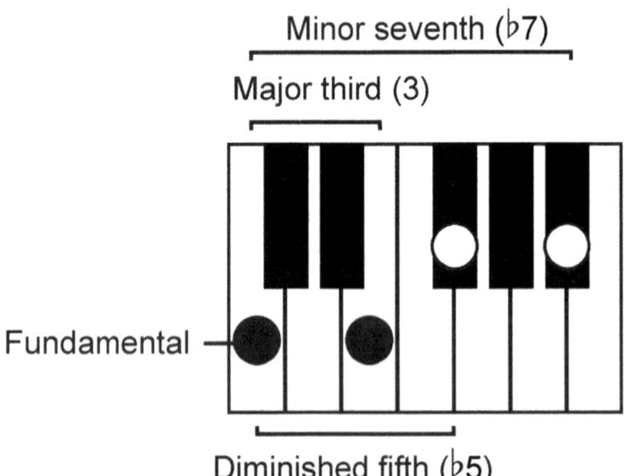

──────── **DOMINANT SEVENTH FLAT NINE** ────────

We add the minor ninth to a minor seventh chord (Dominant).

Notation	Chord name	Interval formula
C7($\flat$9)	**C dominant seventh flat nine**	**1 - 3 - 5 - $\flat$7 - $\flat$9**

- The first letter of the notation (**C**) determines the chord's root note.

- The **7** indicates that the chord includes a minor seventh.

- The ($\flat$**9**) symbol shows that the ninth is minor.

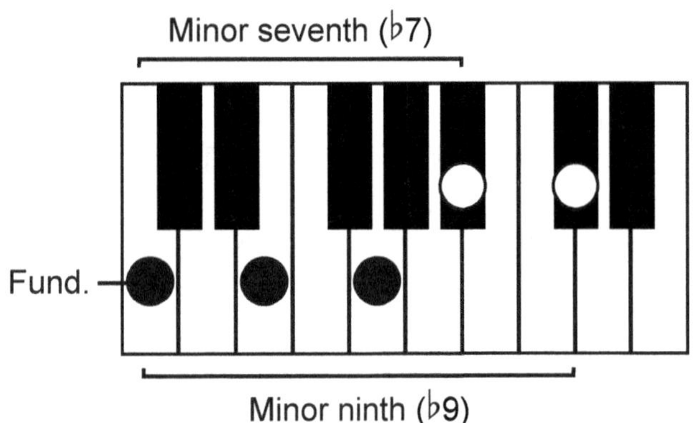

ALTERED CHORD

This is a major chord with a minor seventh where we add an augmented ninth.

Notation	Chord name	Interval formula
C7(♯9)	C altered	1 - 3 - 5 - ♭7 - ♯9

- The **C** corresponds to the root.

- The **7** indicates that the chord includes a minor seventh.

- The (**♯9**) symbol shows that the ninth is augmented.

- This chord is also called C seventh sharp nine.

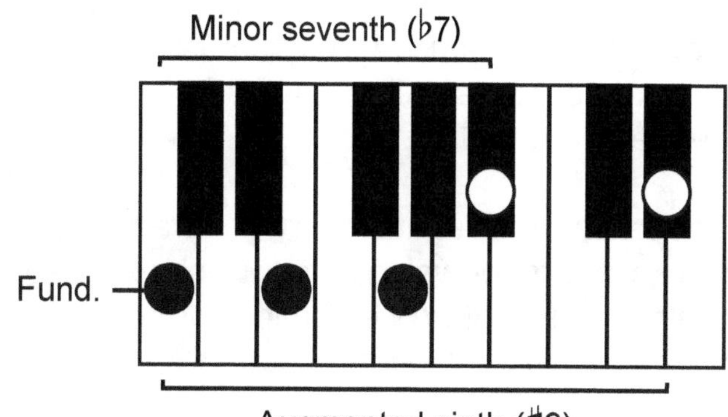

INVERSIONS

The notes in a single chord can be played in different positions on the keyboard, and the note that is in the lowest spot will give the name to that position or inversion.

In the notation, the inversion is shown by using a slash (/) and then indicating which note holds the lowest spot, except in the first root position, where the lowest note gives the chord its name.

C7

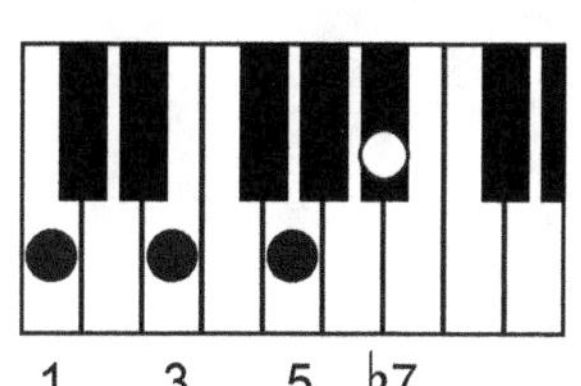

Root position
The lowest note is the root, and that gives the chord its name.

C7/E

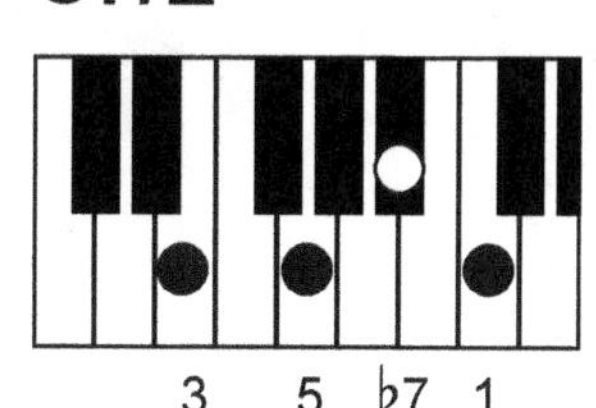

1st inversion
The lowest note is the chord's third. In the case of suspended chords, it is the note that replaces the third.

C7/G

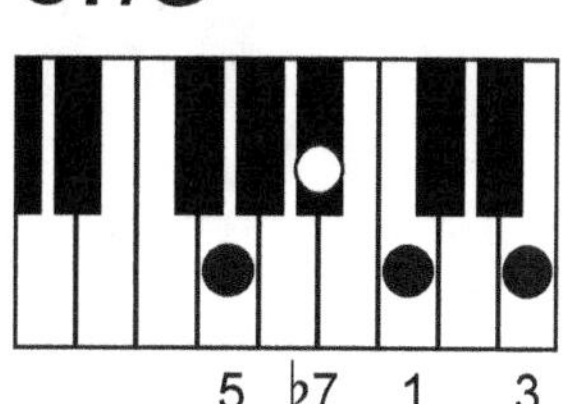

2nd inversion
The lowest note is the chord's fifth.

C7/B♭

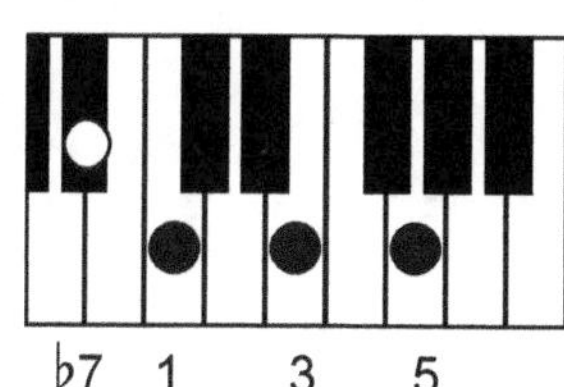

3rd inversion
The lowest note is the chord's sixth or seventh.

VOICINGS

Notations (and the illustrations we've included in this book) only indicate what notes are included in the chord and, in the case of inversions, which is the lowest note of the chord. This doesn't give us information about how to arrange them on the keyboard. That's why we can freely choose which octave to play each of the notes (or voices) in when we work with notation, as well as whether we play them all in order of overlapping thirds or move one of them to a higher or lower location.

However, experience will teach us that as we get closer to the lower end of the keyboard, it isn't best to play all the notes in the chord in that area because the sound becomes too dense and muddled.

The following illustration very generally shows the best way to arrange the chord's voices on the keyboard, or which notes we should play in each area. You'll see that, in general, as the register gets higher, we can include notes that are further away from the chord's basic triad.

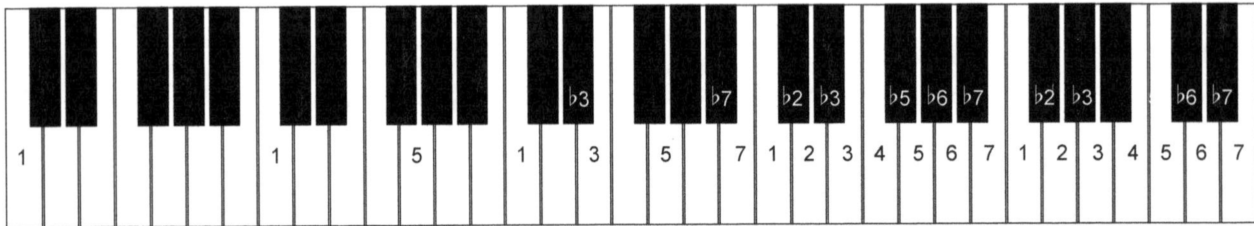

CHORDS TYPES

These are the types of chords most commonly used and presented in this book, along with their notation and the intervals that make them up.

NOTATION	TYPE OF CHORD	INTERVAL FORMULA
TRIADS		
Cm	minor	1 - ♭3 - 5
C	Major	1 - 3 - 5
C°	Diminished	1 - ♭3 - ♭5
C+	Augmented	1 - 3 - ♯5
ALTERED THIRDS		
C5	Fifth (with omitted third (Power chord))	1 - 5
Csus2	Suspended Second Chord	1 - 2 - 5
Csus4	Suspended Fourth Chord	1 - 4 - 5
SEVENTH CHORDS		
Cmaj7	Major Seventh	1 - 3 - 5 - 7
Cm7	Minor Seventh	1 - ♭3 - 5 - ♭7
Cmaj7	Major Seventh	1 - 3 - 5 - 7
C7	Dominant Seventh	1 - 3 - 5 - ♭7
Cm7(♭5)	Half-diminished Seventh	1 - ♭3 - ♭5 - ♭7
C°7	Diminished Seventh	1 - ♭3 - ♭5 - ♭♭7
Cmaj7(♯5)	Augmented Major Seventh	1 - 3 - ♯5 - 7
C+7	Augmented seventh	1 - 3 - ♯5 - ♭7
TRIADS WITH EXTENSIONS		
Cm(add4)	Minor Added-fourth	1 - ♭3 - 4 - 5
Cadd9	Added-ninth	1 - 3 - 5 - 9
Cm(add9)	Minor Added-ninth	1 - ♭3 - 5 - 9
C6	Major Sixth	1 - 3 - 5 - 6
Cm6	Minor Sixth	1 - ♭3 - 5 - 6
SEVENTH CHORDS WITH EXTENSIONS		
Cmaj9	Major Ninth	1 - 3 - 5 - 7 - 9
C9	Dominant Ninth Chord	1 - 3 - 5 - ♭7 - 9
Cm9	Minor Ninth Chord	1 - ♭3 - 5 - ♭7 - 9
C11	Dominant Eleventh Chord	1 - (3) - 5 - ♭7 - 9 - 11
Cm11	Minor Eleventh Chord	1 - ♭3 - 5 - ♭7 - 9 - 11
C13	Dominant Thirteenth Chord	1 - 3 - 5 - ♭7 - 9 - (11) - 13
C7sus4	Seventh Suspended Four Chord	1 - 4 - 5 - ♭7
C7(♭5)	Dominant Seventh Flat Five	1 - 3 - ♭5 - ♭7
C7(♭9)	Dominant Seventh Flat Nine	1 - 3 - 5 - ♭7 - ♭9
C7(♯9)	Altered Chord	1 - 3 - 5 - ♭7 - ♯9

( ) The notes in parentheses can omitted.

C

C
(Root position)
1 3 5

C/E
(1° Inversion)
3 5 1

C/G
(2° Inversion)
5 3 1

Cm
(Root position)
1 ♭3 5

Cm/E♭
(1° Inversion)
♭3 5 1

Cm/G
(2° Inversion)
5 1 ♭3

C+
1 3 ♯5

C°
1 ♭3 ♭5

C5
1 5

Csus2
1 2 5

Csus4
1 4 5

Cmaj7
1 3 5 7

C7
(Root position)
1 3 5 ♭7

C7/E
(1° Inversion)
3 5 ♭7 1

C7/G
(2° Inversion)
5 ♭7 1 3

C7/B♭
(3° Inversion)
♭7 1 3 5

Cm(maj7)
1 ♭3 5 7

Cm7
(Root position)
1 ♭3 5 ♭7

Cm7/E♭
(1° Inversion)
♭3 5 ♭7 1

Cm7/G
(2° Inversion)
5 ♭7 1 ♭3

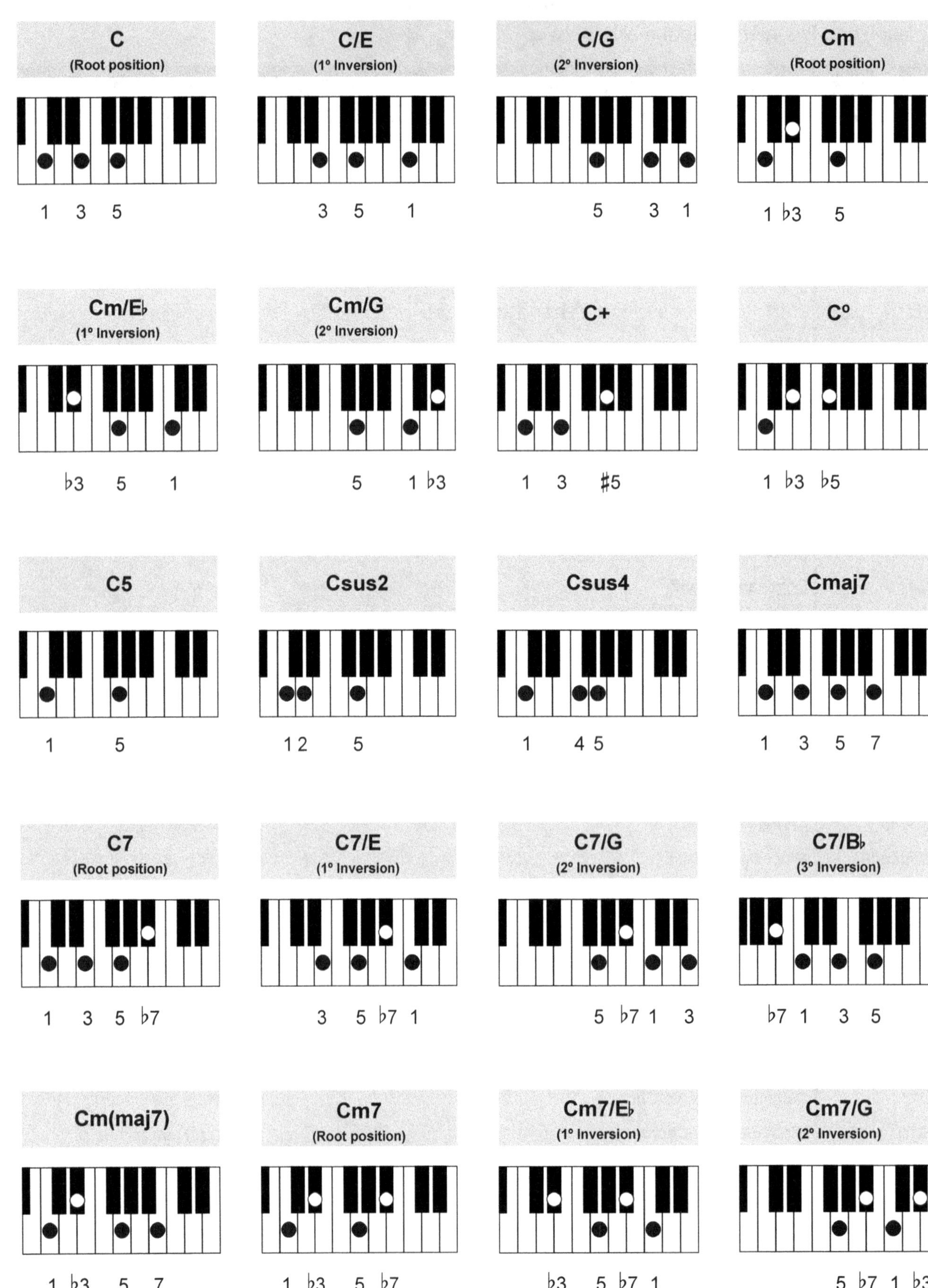

C

Cm7/B♭
(3° Inversion)
♭7 1 ♭3 5

Cm7(♭5)
1 ♭3 ♭5 ♭7

C°7
1 ♭3 ♭5 ♭♭7

Cmaj7(#5)
1 ♭3 #5 7

C+7
1 3 #5 ♭7

Cm(add4)
1 ♭3 4 5

Cadd9
1 2 3 5 9

Cm(add9)
1 2 ♭3 5 9

C6
1 3 5 6

Cm6
1 ♭3 5 6

Cmaj9
1 2 3 5 7 9

C9
1 2 3 5 ♭7 9

Cm9
1 2 ♭3 5 ♭7 9

C11
1 3 5 ♭7 9 11

Cm11
1 ♭3 5 ♭7 9 11

C13
1 3 5 ♭7 9 11 13

C7sus4
1 4 5 ♭7

C7(♭5)
1 3 ♭5 ♭7

C7(♭9)
1 3 5 ♭7 ♭9

C7(#9)
1 3 5 ♭7 #9

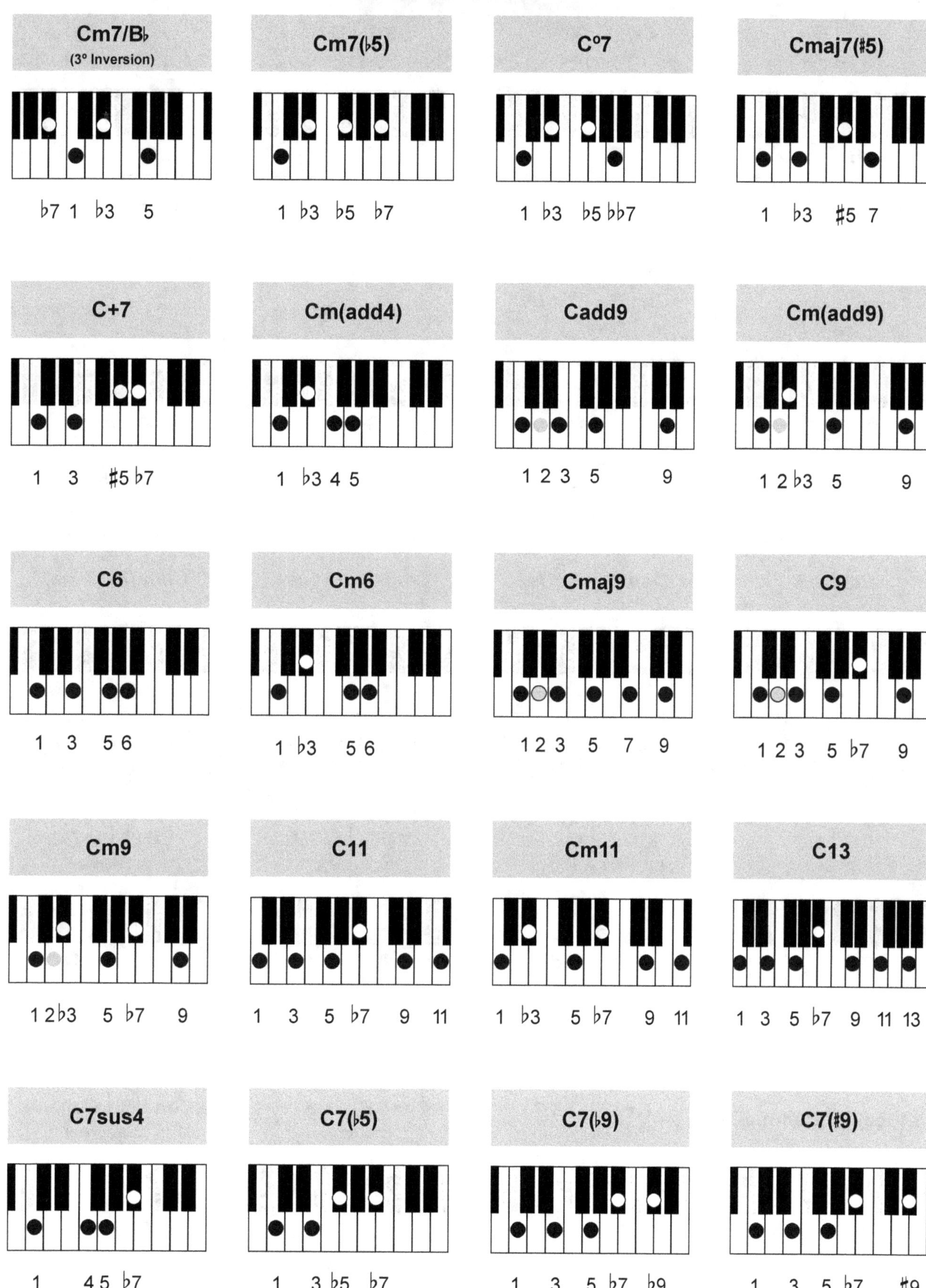

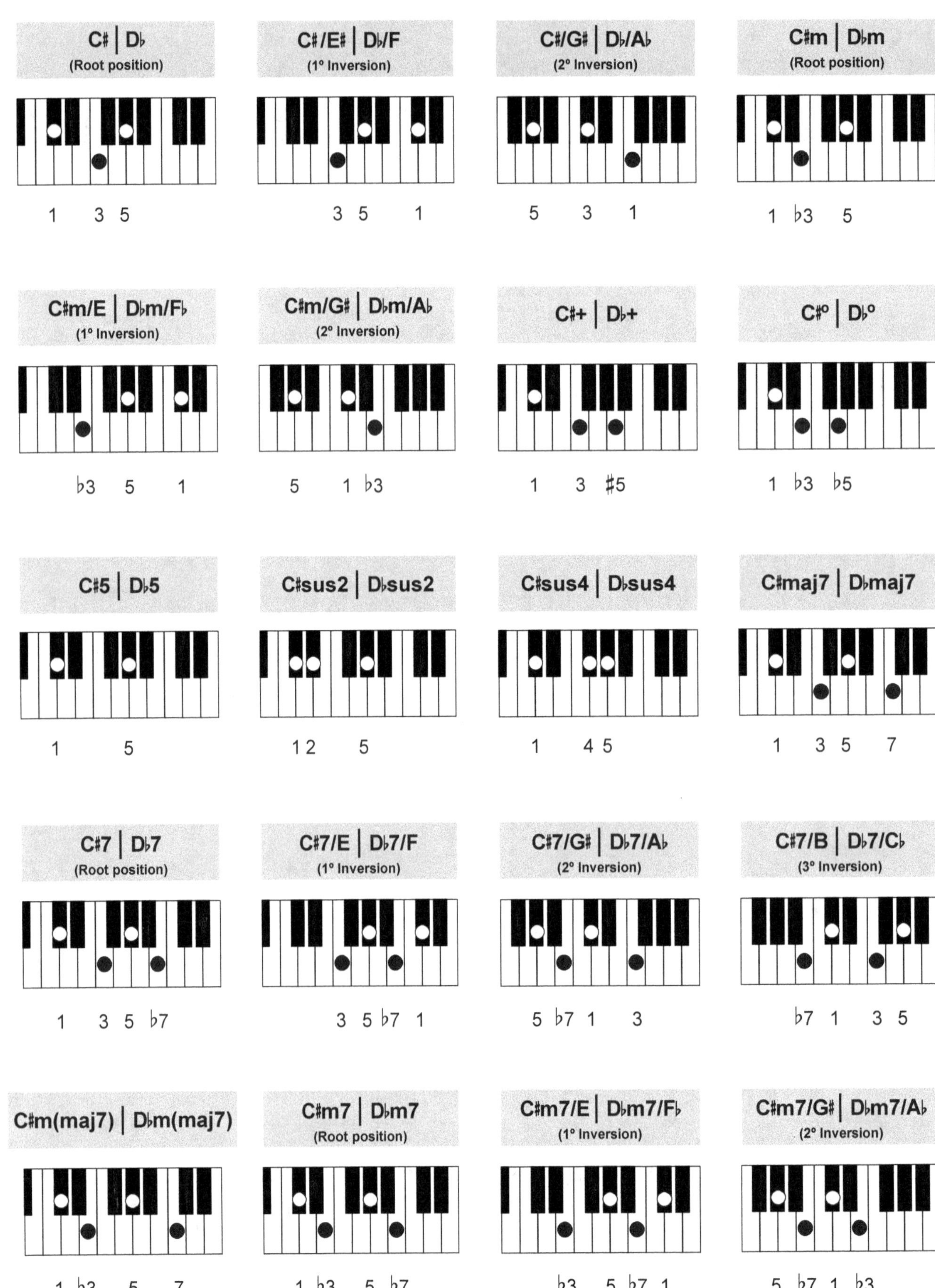

C# | Db
C# | Db
(Root position)
1 3 5

C#/E# | Db/F
(1° Inversion)
3 5 1

C#/G# | Db/Ab
(2° Inversion)
5 3 1

C#m | Dbm
(Root position)
1 b3 5

C#m/E | Dbm/Fb
(1° Inversion)
b3 5 1

C#m/G# | Dbm/Ab
(2° Inversion)
5 1 b3

C#+ | Db+
1 3 #5

C#° | Db°
1 b3 b5

C#5 | Db5
1 5

C#sus2 | Dbsus2
1 2 5

C#sus4 | Dbsus4
1 4 5

C#maj7 | Dbmaj7
1 3 5 7

C#7 | Db7
(Root position)
1 3 5 b7

C#7/E | Db7/F
(1° Inversion)
3 5 b7 1

C#7/G# | Db7/Ab
(2° Inversion)
5 b7 1 3

C#7/B | Db7/Cb
(3° Inversion)
b7 1 3 5

C#m(maj7) | Dbm(maj7)
1 b3 5 7

C#m7 | Dbm7
(Root position)
1 b3 5 b7

C#m7/E | Dbm7/Fb
(1° Inversion)
b3 5 b7 1

C#m7/G# | Dbm7/Ab
(2° Inversion)
5 b7 1 b3

C# | D♭

C#m7/B | D♭m7/C♭
(3° Inversion)
♭7 1 ♭3 5

C#m7(♭5) | D♭m7(♭5)
1 ♭3 ♭5 ♭7

C#°7 | D♭°7
1 ♭3 ♭5 ♭♭7

C#maj7(#5) | D♭maj7(#5)
1 ♭3 #5 7

C#+7 | D♭+7
1 3 #5 ♭7

C#m(add4) | D♭m(add4)
1 ♭3 4 5

C#add9 | D♭add9
1 2 3 5 9

C#m(add9) | D♭m(add9)
1 2 ♭3 5 9

C#6 | D♭6
1 3 5 6

C#m6 | D♭m6
1 ♭3 5 6

C#maj9 | D♭maj9
1 2 3 5 7 9

C#9 | D♭9
1 2 3 5 ♭7 9

C#m9 | D♭m9
1 2 ♭3 5 ♭7 9

C#11 | D♭11
1 3 5 ♭7 9 11

C#m11 | D♭m11
1 ♭3 5 ♭7 9 11

C#13 | D♭13
1 3 5 ♭7 9 11 13

C#7sus4 | D♭7sus4
1 4 5 ♭7

C#7(♭5) | D♭7(♭5)
1 3 ♭5 ♭7

C#7(♭9) | D♭7(♭9)
1 3 5 ♭7 ♭9

C#7(#9) | D♭7(#9)
1 3 5 ♭7 #9

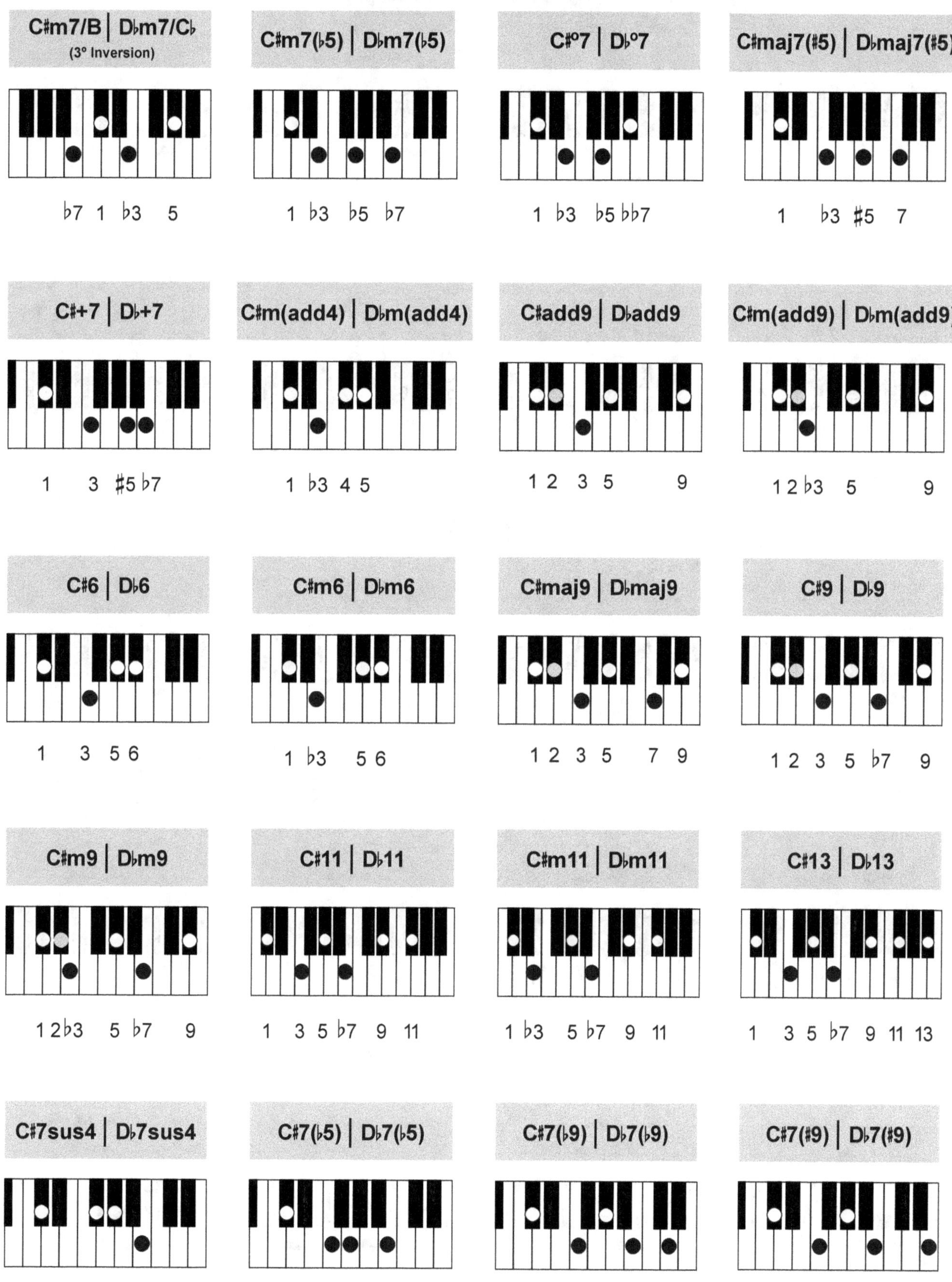

D

D
(Root position)
1 3 5

D/F♯
(1º Inversion)
3 5 1

D/A
(2º Inversion)
5 3 1

Dm
(Root position)
1 ♭3 5

Dm/F
(1º Inversion)
♭3 5 1

Dm/A
(2º Inversion)
5 1 ♭3

D+
1 3 ♯5

Dº
1 ♭3 ♭5

D5
1 5

Dsus2
1 2 5

Dsus4
1 4 5

Dmaj7
1 3 5 7

D7
(Root position)
1 3 5 ♭7

D7/F♯
(1º Inversion)
3 5 ♭7 1

D7/A
(2º Inversion)
5 ♭7 1 3

D7/C
(3º Inversion)
♭7 1 3 5

Dm(maj7)
1 ♭3 5 7

Dm7
(Root position)
1 ♭3 5 ♭7

Dm7/F
(1º Inversion)
♭3 5 ♭7 1

Dm7/A
(2º Inversion)
5 ♭7 1 ♭3

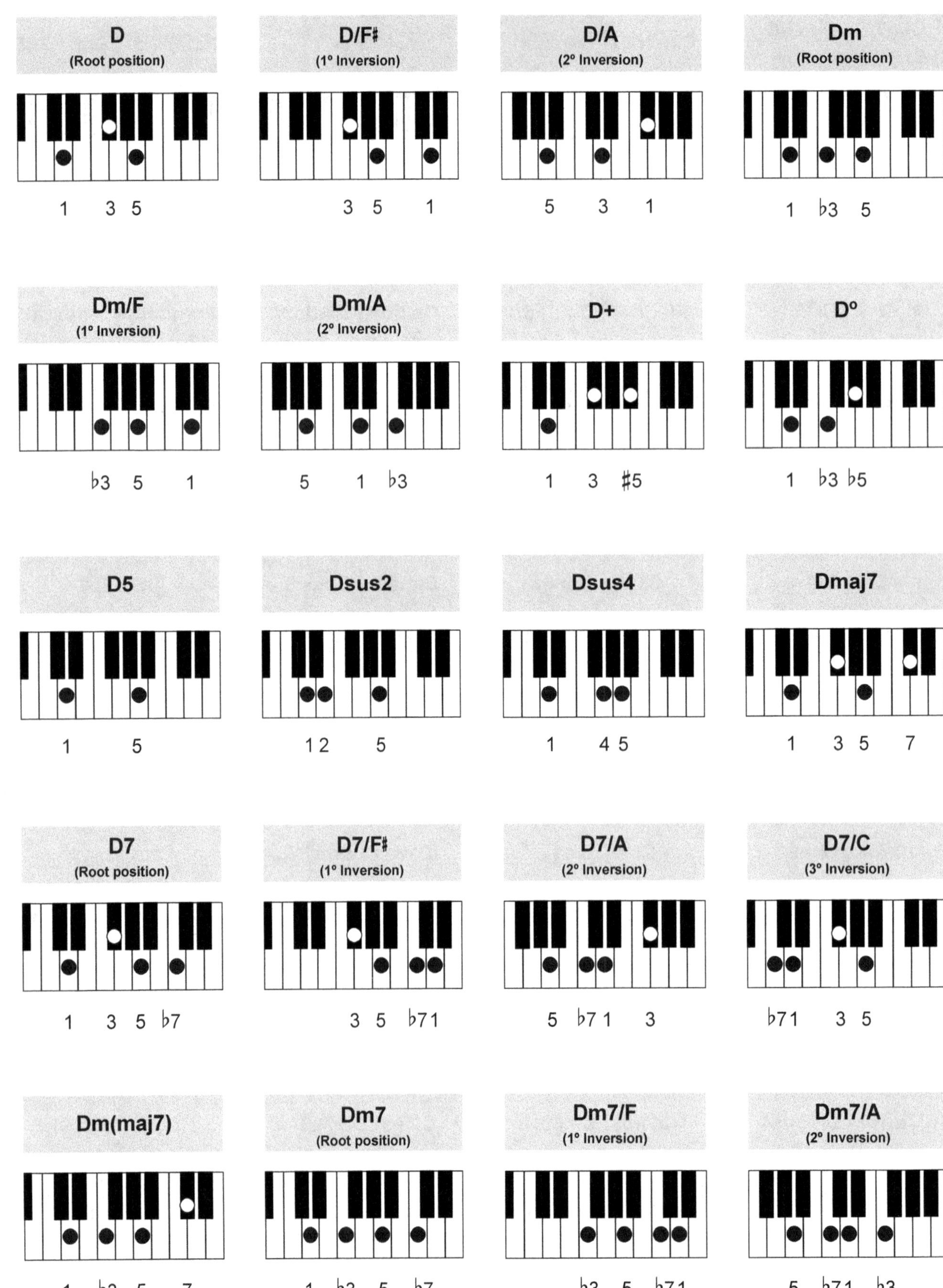

D

Dm7/C
(3º Inversion)
♭7 1 ♭3 5

Dm7(♭5)
1 ♭3 ♭5 ♭7

Dº7
1 ♭3 ♭5 ♭♭7

Dmaj7(♯5)
1 ♭3 ♯5 7

D+7
1 3 ♯5 ♭7

Dm(add4)
1 ♭3 4 5

Dadd9
1 2 3 5 9

Dm(add9)
1 2 ♭3 5 9

D6
1 3 5 6

Dm6
1 ♭3 5 6

Dmaj9
1 2 3 5 7 9

D9
1 2 3 5 ♭7 9

Dm9
1 2 ♭3 5 ♭7 9

D11
1 3 5 ♭7 9 11

Dm11
1 ♭3 5 ♭7 9 11

D13
1 3 5 ♭7 9 11 13

D7sus4
1 4 5 ♭7

D7(♭5)
1 3 ♭5 ♭7

D7(♭9)
1 3 5 ♭7 ♭9

D7(♯9)
1 3 5 ♭7 ♯9

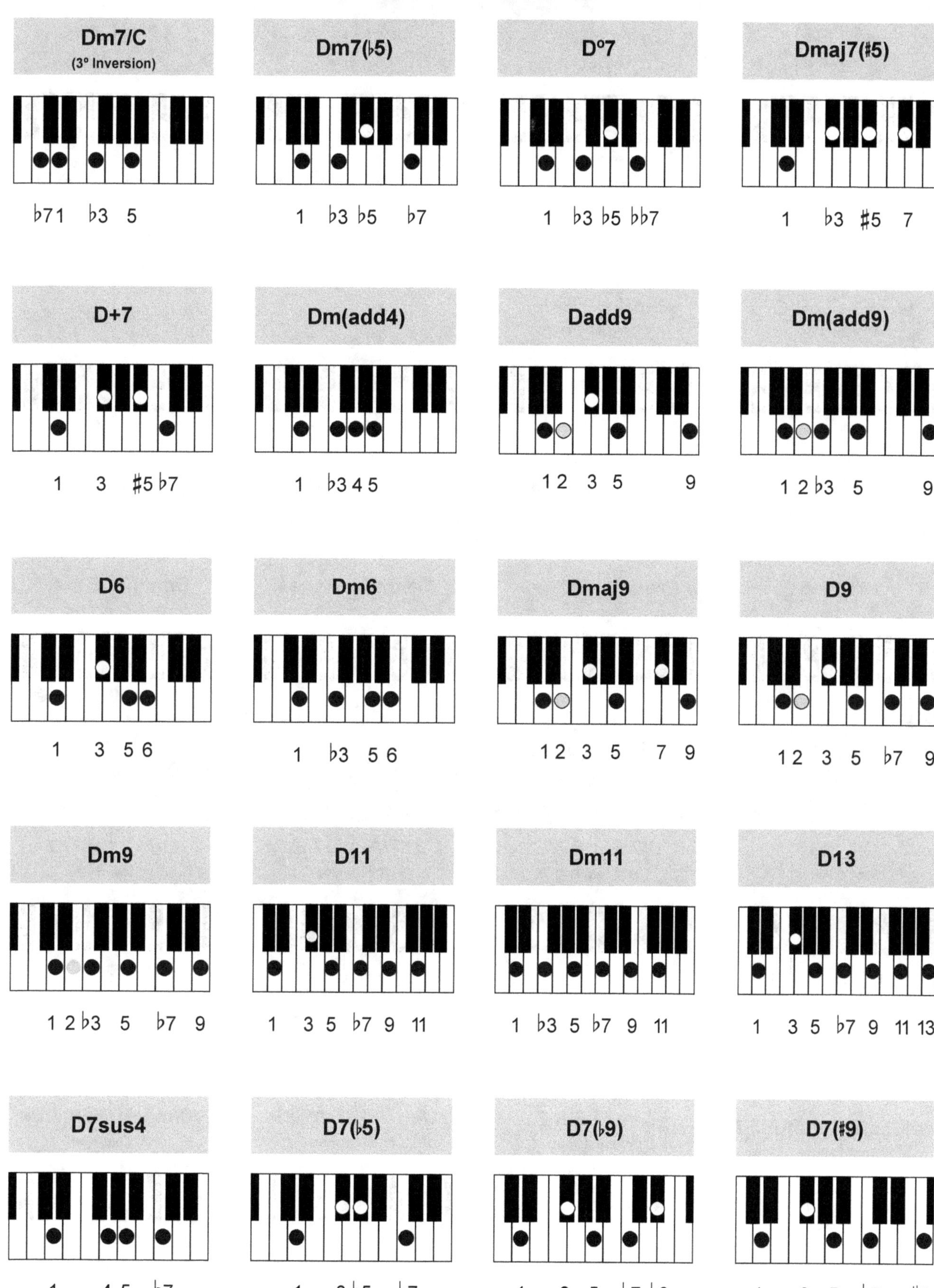

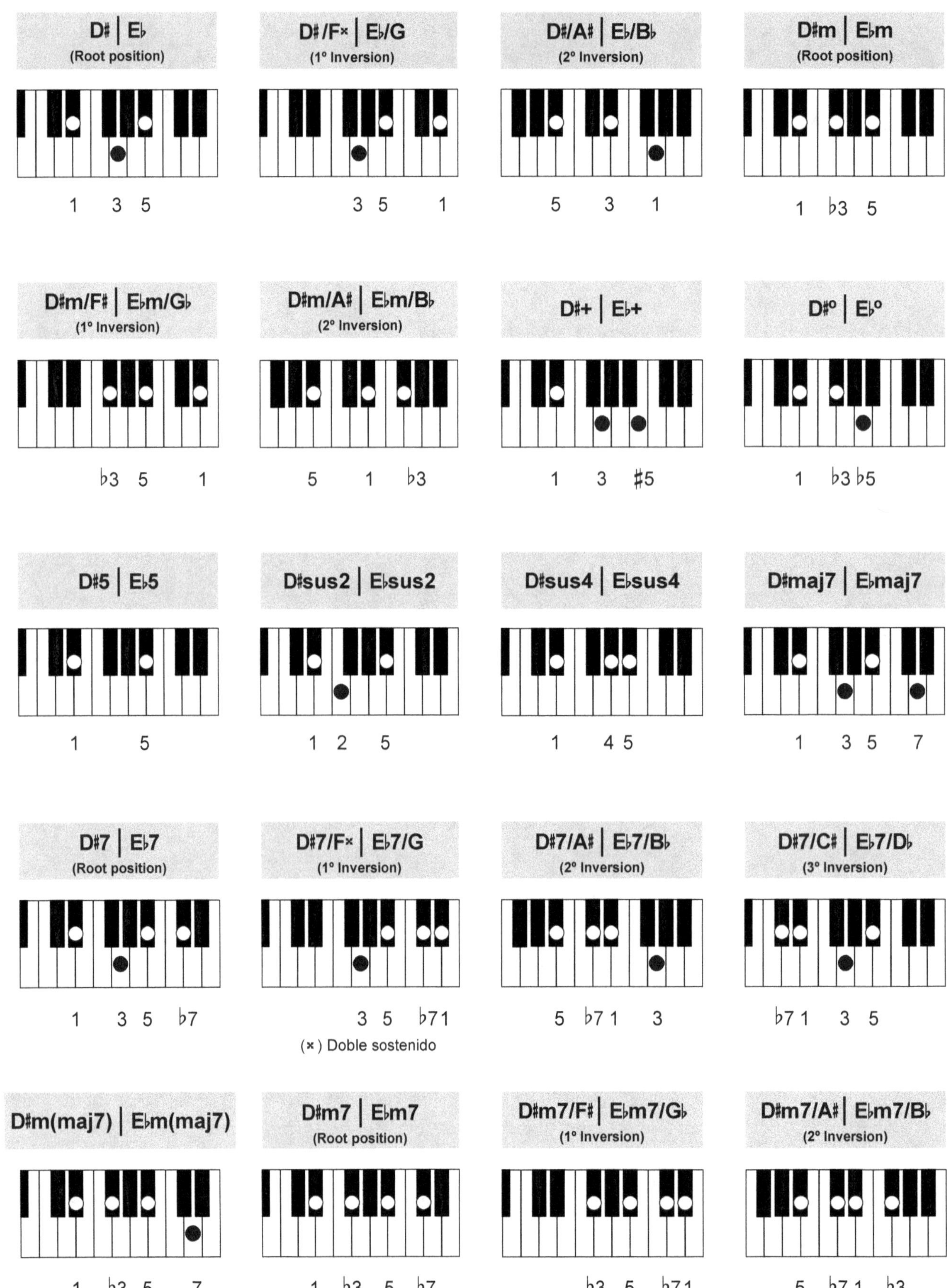

D# | E♭
(Root position)
1 3 5

D#/F× | E♭/G
(1º Inversion)
3 5 1

D#/A# | E♭/B♭
(2º Inversion)
5 3 1

D#m | E♭m
(Root position)
1 ♭3 5

D#m/F# | E♭m/G♭
(1º Inversion)
♭3 5 1

D#m/A# | E♭m/B♭
(2º Inversion)
5 1 ♭3

D#+ | E♭+
1 3 #5

D#º | E♭º
1 ♭3 ♭5

D#5 | E♭5
1 5

D#sus2 | E♭sus2
1 2 5

D#sus4 | E♭sus4
1 4 5

D#maj7 | E♭maj7
1 3 5 7

D#7 | E♭7
(Root position)
1 3 5 ♭7

D#7/F× | E♭7/G
(1º Inversion)
3 5 ♭7 1

D#7/A# | E♭7/B♭
(2º Inversion)
5 ♭7 1 3

D#7/C# | E♭7/D♭
(3º Inversion)
♭7 1 3 5

(×) Doble sostenido

D#m(maj7) | E♭m(maj7)
1 ♭3 5 7

D#m7 | E♭m7
(Root position)
1 ♭3 5 ♭7

D#m7/F# | E♭m7/G♭
(1º Inversion)
♭3 5 ♭7 1

D#m7/A# | E♭m7/B♭
(2º Inversion)
5 ♭7 1 ♭3

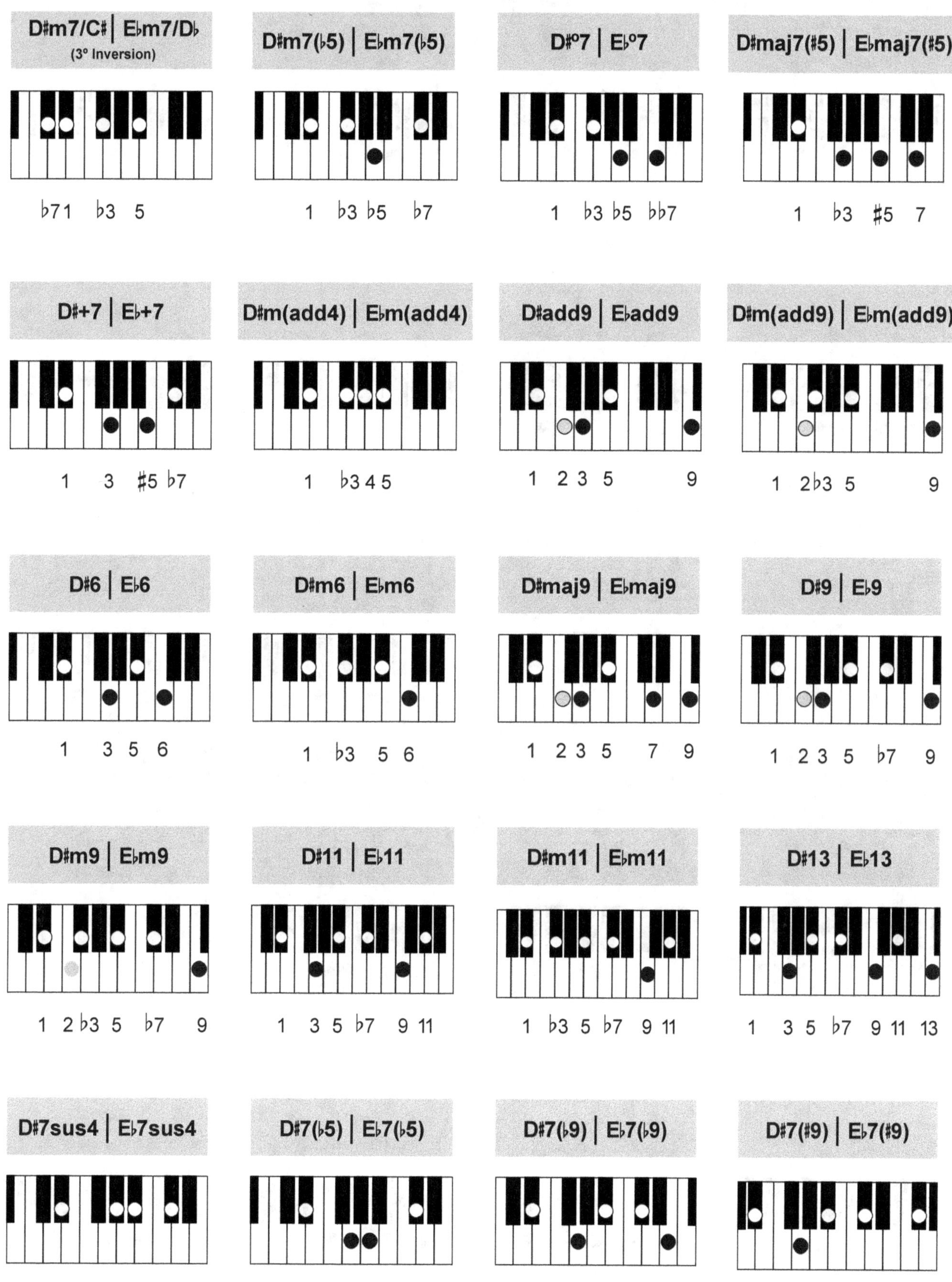

D♯m7/C♯ | E♭m7/D♭
(3º Inversion)
♭7 1   ♭3   5

D♯m7(♭5) | E♭m7(♭5)
1   ♭3 ♭5   ♭7

D♯º7 | E♭º7
1   ♭3 ♭5   ♭♭7

D♯maj7(♯5) | E♭maj7(♯5)
1   ♭3   ♯5   7

D♯+7 | E♭+7
1   3   ♯5 ♭7

D♯m(add4) | E♭m(add4)
1   ♭3 4 5

D♯add9 | E♭add9
1   2 3   5   9

D♯m(add9) | E♭m(add9)
1   2♭3   5   9

D♯6 | E♭6
1   3 5 6

D♯m6 | E♭m6
1   ♭3   5 6

D♯maj9 | E♭maj9
1   2 3   5   7   9

D♯9 | E♭9
1   2 3   5   ♭7   9

D♯m9 | E♭m9
1   2♭3   5   ♭7   9

D♯11 | E♭11
1   3 5   ♭7   9 11

D♯m11 | E♭m11
1   ♭3   5   ♭7   9 11

D♯13 | E♭13
1   3 5   ♭7   9 11 13

D♯7sus4 | E♭7sus4
1   4 5   ♭7

D♯7(♭5) | E♭7(♭5)
1   3 ♭5   ♭7

D♯7(♭9) | E♭7(♭9)
1   3 5   ♭7 ♭9

D♯7(♯9) | E♭7(♯9)
1   3 5   ♭7   ♯9

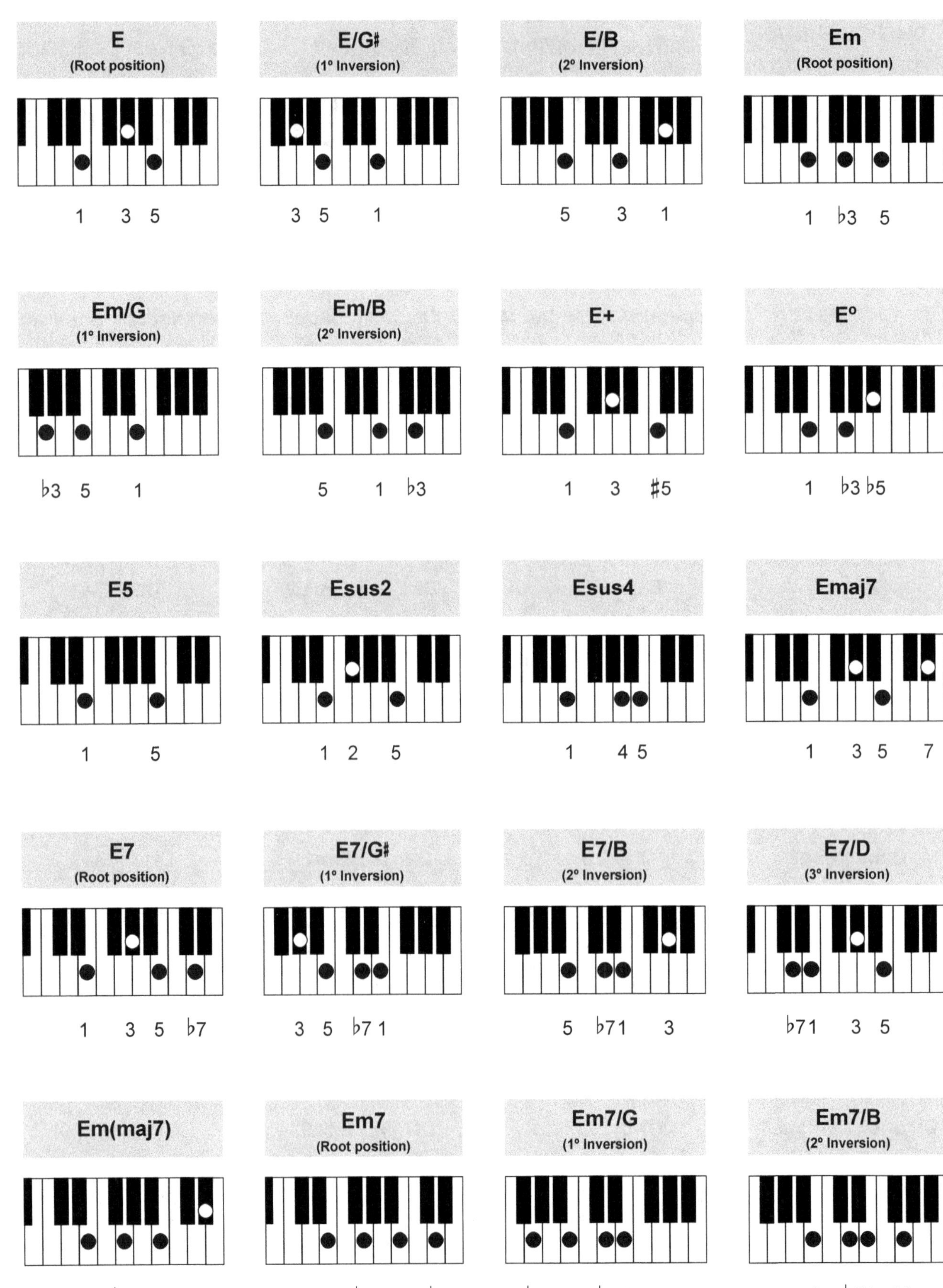

E (Root position) — 1 3 5

E/G♯ (1° Inversion) — 3 5 1

E/B (2° Inversion) — 5 3 1

Em (Root position) — 1 ♭3 5

Em/G (1° Inversion) — ♭3 5 1

Em/B (2° Inversion) — 5 1 ♭3

E+ — 1 3 ♯5

E° — 1 ♭3 ♭5

E5 — 1 5

Esus2 — 1 2 5

Esus4 — 1 4 5

Emaj7 — 1 3 5 7

E7 (Root position) — 1 3 5 ♭7

E7/G♯ (1° Inversion) — 3 5 ♭7 1

E7/B (2° Inversion) — 5 ♭7 1 3

E7/D (3° Inversion) — ♭7 1 3 5

Em(maj7) — 1 ♭3 5 7

Em7 (Root position) — 1 ♭3 5 ♭7

Em7/G (1° Inversion) — ♭3 5 ♭7 1

Em7/B (2° Inversion) — 5 ♭7 1 ♭3

E

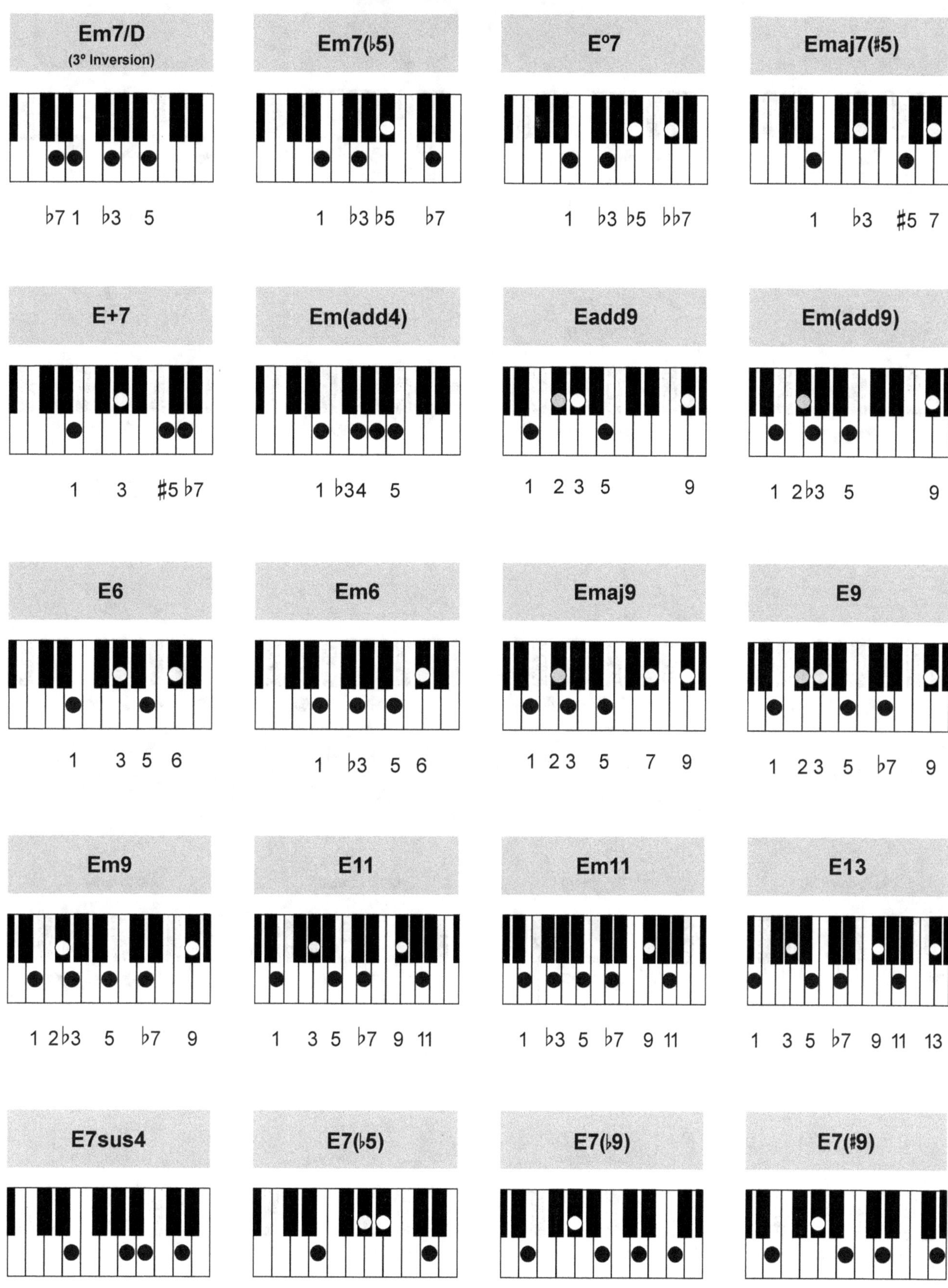

F

F
(Root position)
1 3 5

F/A
(1º Inversion)
3 5 1

F/C
(2º Inversion)
5 3 1

Fm
(Root position)
1 ♭3 5

Fm/A♭
(1º Inversion)
♭3 5 1

Fm/C
(2º Inversion)
5 1 ♭3

F+
1 3 ♯5

Fº
1 ♭3 ♭5

F5
1 5

Fsus2
1 2 5

Fsus4
1 4 5

Fmaj7
1 3 5 7

F7
(Root position)
1 3 5 ♭7

F7/A
(1º Inversion)
3 5 ♭7 1

F7/C
(2º Inversion)
5 ♭7 1 3

F7/E♭
(3º Inversion)
♭7 1 3 5

Fm(maj7)
1 ♭3 5 7

Fm7
(Root position)
1 ♭3 5 ♭7

Fm7/A♭
(1º Inversion)
♭3 5 ♭7 1

Fm7/C
(2º Inversion)
5 ♭7 1 ♭3

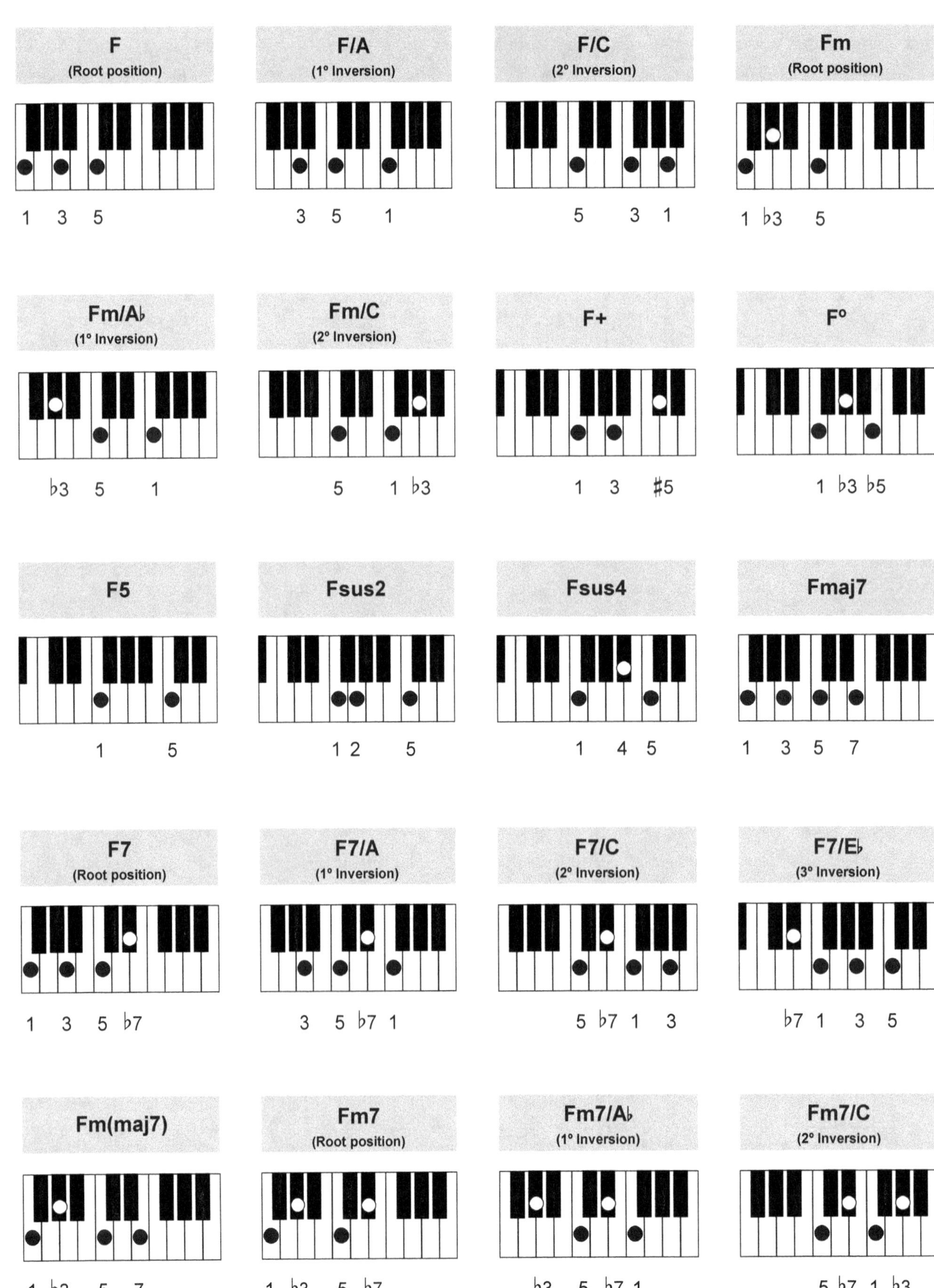

F

Fm7/E♭
(3° Inversion)
♭7 1 ♭3 5

Fm7(♭5)
1 ♭3 ♭5 ♭7

F°7
1 ♭3 ♭5 ♭♭7

Fmaj7(♯5)
1 ♭3 ♯5 7

F+7
1 3 ♯5 ♭7

Fm(add4)
1 ♭3 4 5

Fadd9
1 2 3 5 9

Fm(add9)
1 2 ♭3 5 9

F6
1 3 5 6

Fm6
1 ♭3 5 6

Fmaj9
1 2 3 5 7 9

F9
1 2 3 5 ♭7 9

Fm9
1 2 ♭3 5 ♭7 9

F11
1 3 5 ♭7 9 11

Fm11
1 ♭3 5 ♭7 9 11

F13
1 3 5 ♭7 9 11 13

F7sus4
1 4 5 ♭7

F7(♭5)
1 3 ♭5 ♭7

F7(♭9)
1 3 5 ♭7 ♭9

F7(♯9)
1 3 5 ♭7 ♯9

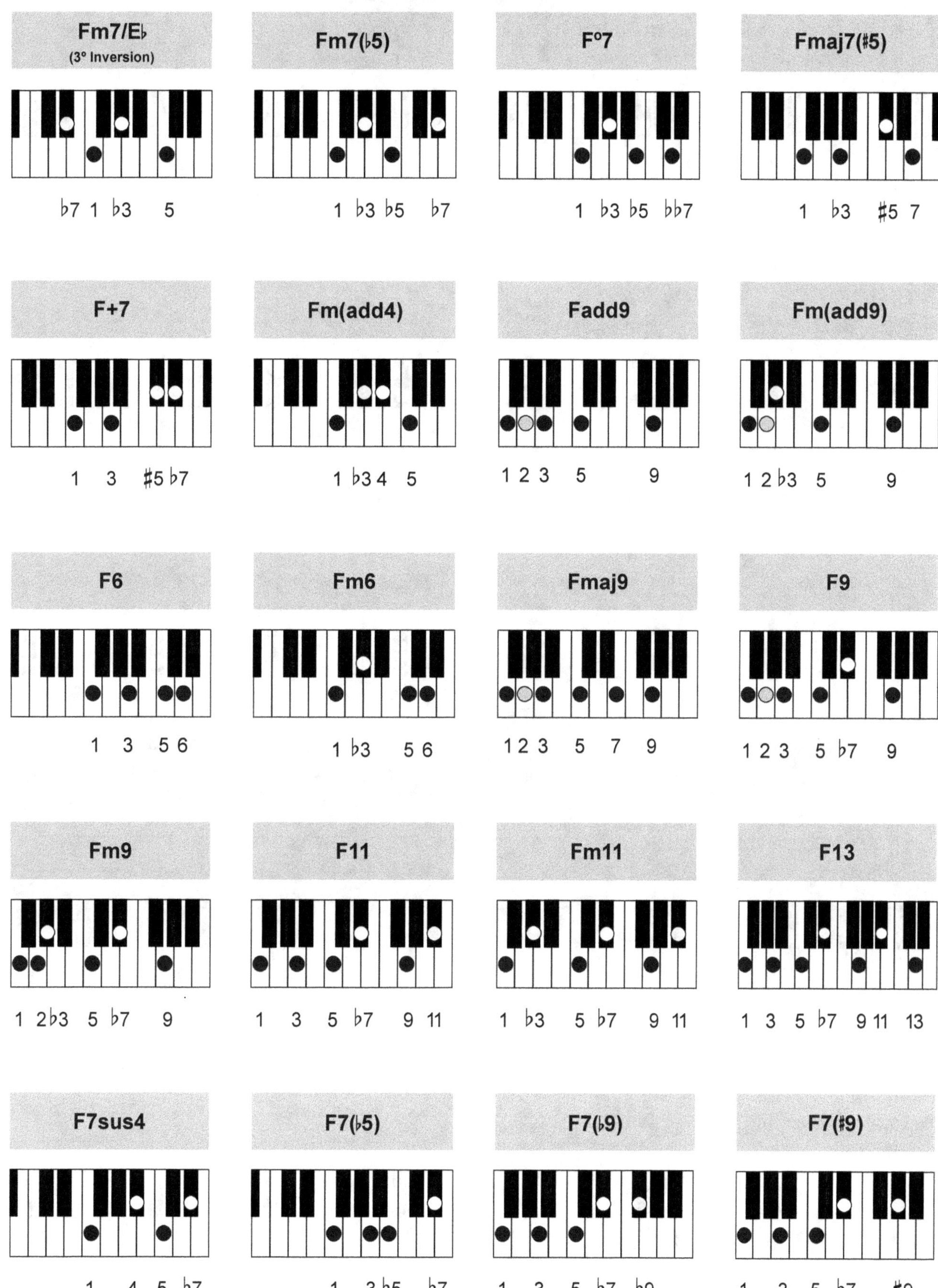

F# | G♭

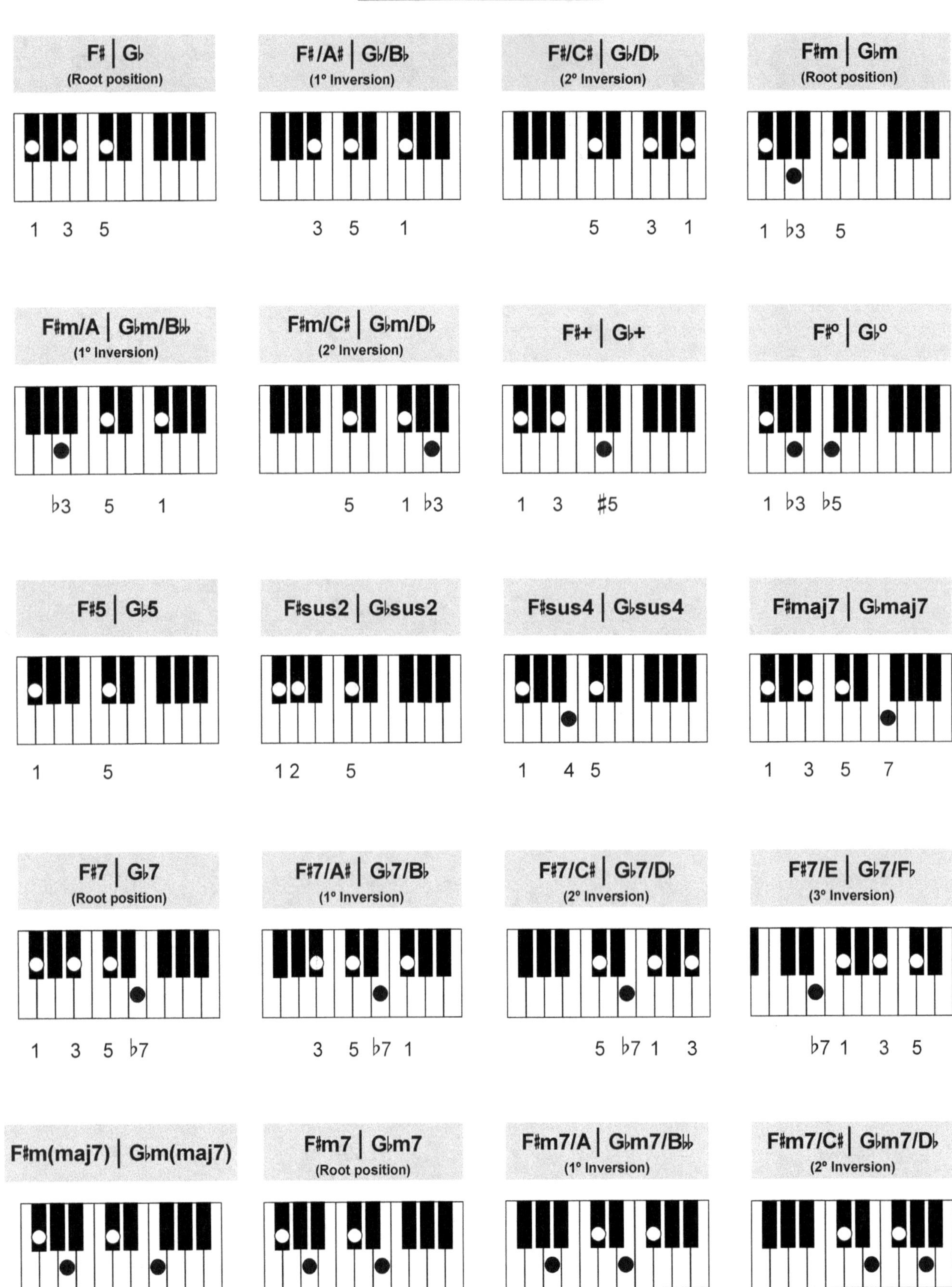

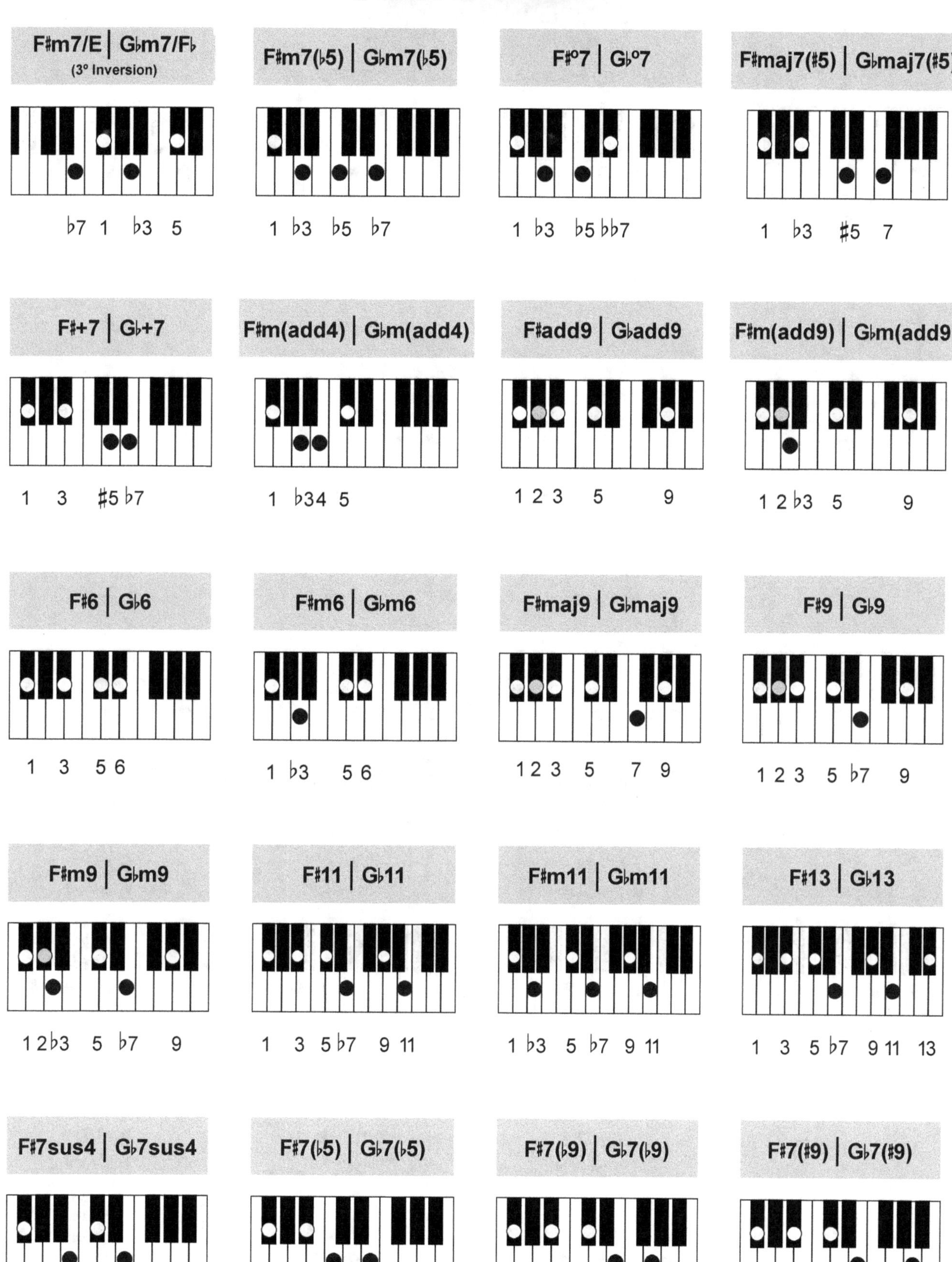

F#m7/E | Gbm7/Fb (3º Inversion)
b7 1 b3 5

F#m7(b5) | Gbm7(b5)
1 b3 b5 b7

F#º7 | Gbº7
1 b3 b5 bb7

F#maj7(#5) | Gbmaj7(#5)
1 b3 #5 7

F#+7 | Gb+7
1 3 #5 b7

F#m(add4) | Gbm(add4)
1 b3 4 5

F#add9 | Gbadd9
1 2 3 5 9

F#m(add9) | Gbm(add9)
1 2 b3 5 9

F#6 | Gb6
1 3 5 6

F#m6 | Gbm6
1 b3 5 6

F#maj9 | Gbmaj9
1 2 3 5 7 9

F#9 | Gb9
1 2 3 5 b7 9

F#m9 | Gbm9
1 2 b3 5 b7 9

F#11 | Gb11
1 3 5 b7 9 11

F#m11 | Gbm11
1 b3 5 b7 9 11

F#13 | Gb13
1 3 5 b7 9 11 13

F#7sus4 | Gb7sus4
1 4 5 b7

F#7(b5) | Gb7(b5)
1 3 b5 b7

F#7(b9) | Gb7(b9)
1 3 5 b7 b9

F#7(#9) | Gb7(#9)
1 3 5 b7 #9

G

G
(Root position)
1 3 5

G/B
(1º Inversion)
3 5 1

G/D
(2º Inversion)
5 3 1

Gm
(Root position)
1 ♭3 5

Gm/B♭
(1º Inversion)
♭3 5 1

Gm/D
(2º Inversion)
5 1 ♭3

G+
1 3 ♯5

Gº
1 ♭3 ♭5

G5
1 5

Gsus2
1 2 5

Gsus4
1 4 5

Gmaj7
1 3 5 7

G7
(Root position)
1 3 5 ♭7

G7/B
(1º Inversion)
3 5 ♭7 1

G7/D
(2º Inversion)
5 ♭7 1 3

G7/F
(3º Inversion)
♭7 1 3 5

Gm(maj7)
1 ♭3 5 7

Gm7
(Root position)
1 ♭3 5 ♭7

Gm7/B♭
(1º Inversion)
♭3 5 ♭7 1

Gm7/D
(2º Inversion)
5 ♭7 1 ♭3

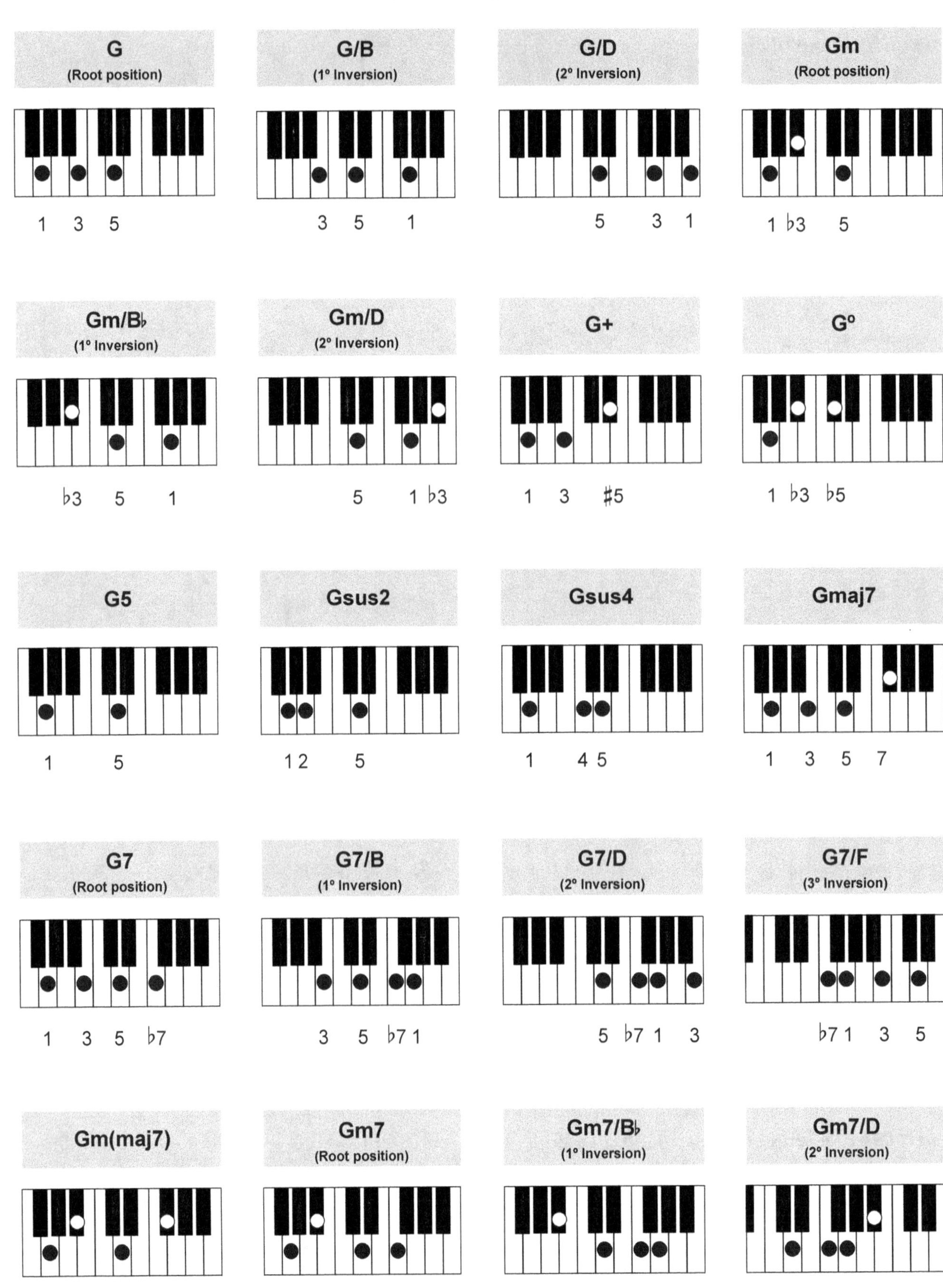

G

Gm7/F
(3° Inversion)
b7 1 b3 5

Gm7(b5)
1 b3 b5 b7

G°7
1 b3 b5 bb7

Gmaj7(#5)
1 b3 #5 7

G+7
1 3 #5 b7

Gm(add4)
1 b3 4 5

Gadd9
1 2 3 5 9

Gm(add9)
1 2 b3 5 9

G6
1 3 5 6

Gm6
1 b3 5 6

Gmaj9
1 2 3 5 7 9

G9
1 2 3 5 b7 9

Gm9
1 2 b3 5 b7 9

G11
1 3 5 b7 9 11

Gm11
1 b3 5 b7 9 11

G13
1 3 5 b7 9 11 13

G7sus4
1 4 5 b7

G7(b5)
1 3 b5 b7

G7(b9)
1 3 5 b7 b9

G7(#9)
1 3 5 b7 #9

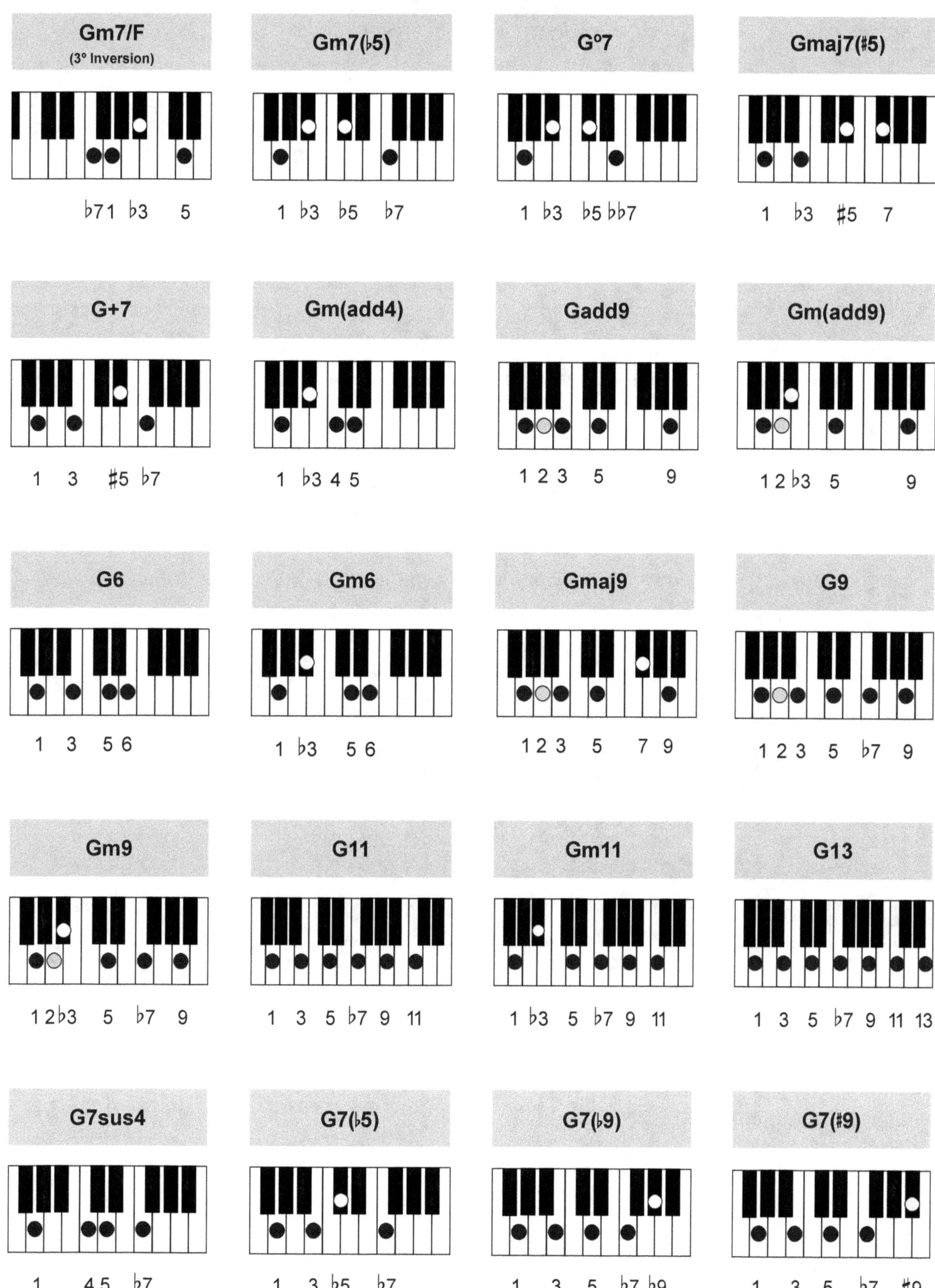

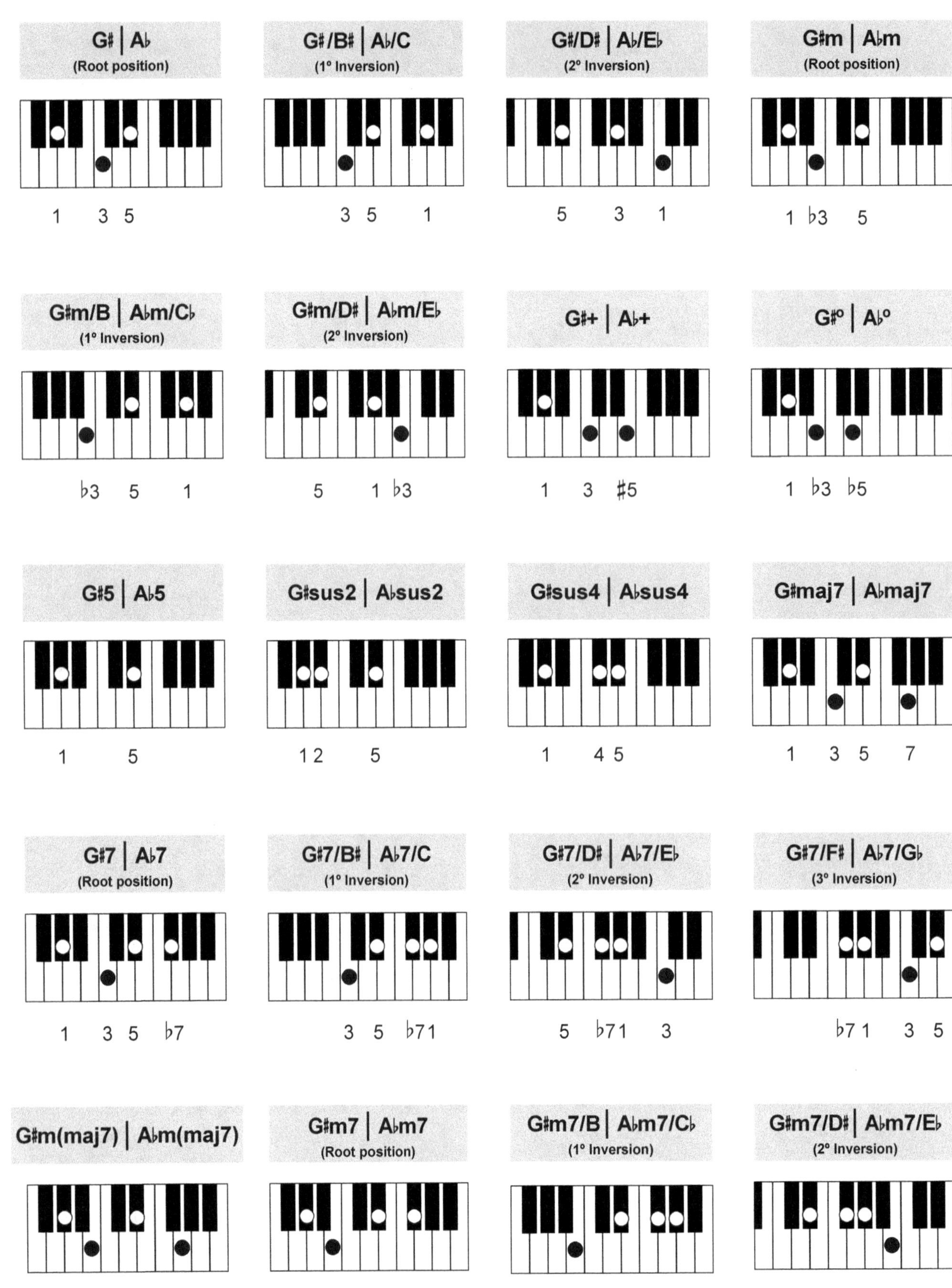

G# | A♭
(Root position)
1 3 5

G#/B# | A♭/C
(1° Inversion)
3 5 1

G#/D# | A♭/E♭
(2° Inversion)
5 3 1

G#m | A♭m
(Root position)
1 ♭3 5

G#m/B | A♭m/C♭
(1° Inversion)
♭3 5 1

G#m/D# | A♭m/E♭
(2° Inversion)
5 1 ♭3

G#+ | A♭+
1 3 #5

G#° | A♭°
1 ♭3 ♭5

G#5 | A♭5
1 5

G#sus2 | A♭sus2
1 2 5

G#sus4 | A♭sus4
1 4 5

G#maj7 | A♭maj7
1 3 5 7

G#7 | A♭7
(Root position)
1 3 5 ♭7

G#7/B# | A♭7/C
(1° Inversion)
3 5 ♭7 1

G#7/D# | A♭7/E♭
(2° Inversion)
5 ♭7 1 3

G#7/F# | A♭7/G♭
(3° Inversion)
♭7 1 3 5

G#m(maj7) | A♭m(maj7)
1 ♭3 5 7

G#m7 | A♭m7
(Root position)
1 ♭3 5 ♭7

G#m7/B | A♭m7/C♭
(1° Inversion)
♭3 5 ♭7 1

G#m7/D# | A♭m7/E♭
(2° Inversion)
5 ♭7 1 ♭3

G♯ | A♭

G♯m7/F♯ | A♭m7/G♭
(3º Inversion)
♭71 ♭3 5

G♯m7(♭5) | A♭m7(♭5)
1 ♭3 ♭5 ♭7

G♯°7 | A♭°7
1 ♭3 ♭5 ♭♭7

G♯maj7(♯5) | A♭maj7(♯5)
1 ♭3 ♯5 7

G♯+7 | A♭+7
1 3 ♯5 ♭7

G♯m(add4) | A♭m(add4)
1 ♭3 4 5

G♯add9 | A♭add9
1 2 3 5 9

G♯m(add9) | A♭m(add9)
1 2 ♭3 5 9

G♯6 | A♭6
1 3 5 6

G♯m6 | A♭m6
1 ♭3 5 6

G♯maj9 | A♭maj9
1 2 3 5 7 9

G♯9 | A♭9
1 2 3 5 ♭7 9

G♯m9 | A♭m9
1 2 ♭3 5 ♭7 9

G♯11 | A♭11
1 3 5 ♭7 9 11

G♯m11 | A♭m11
1 ♭3 5 ♭7 9 11

G♯13 | A♭13
1 3 5 ♭7 9 11 13

G♯7sus4 | A♭7sus4
1 4 5 ♭7

G♯7(♭5) | A♭7(♭5)
1 3 ♭5 ♭7

G♯7(♭9) | A♭7(♭9)
1 3 5 ♭7 ♭9

G♯7(♯9) | A♭7(♯9)
1 3 5 ♭7 ♯9

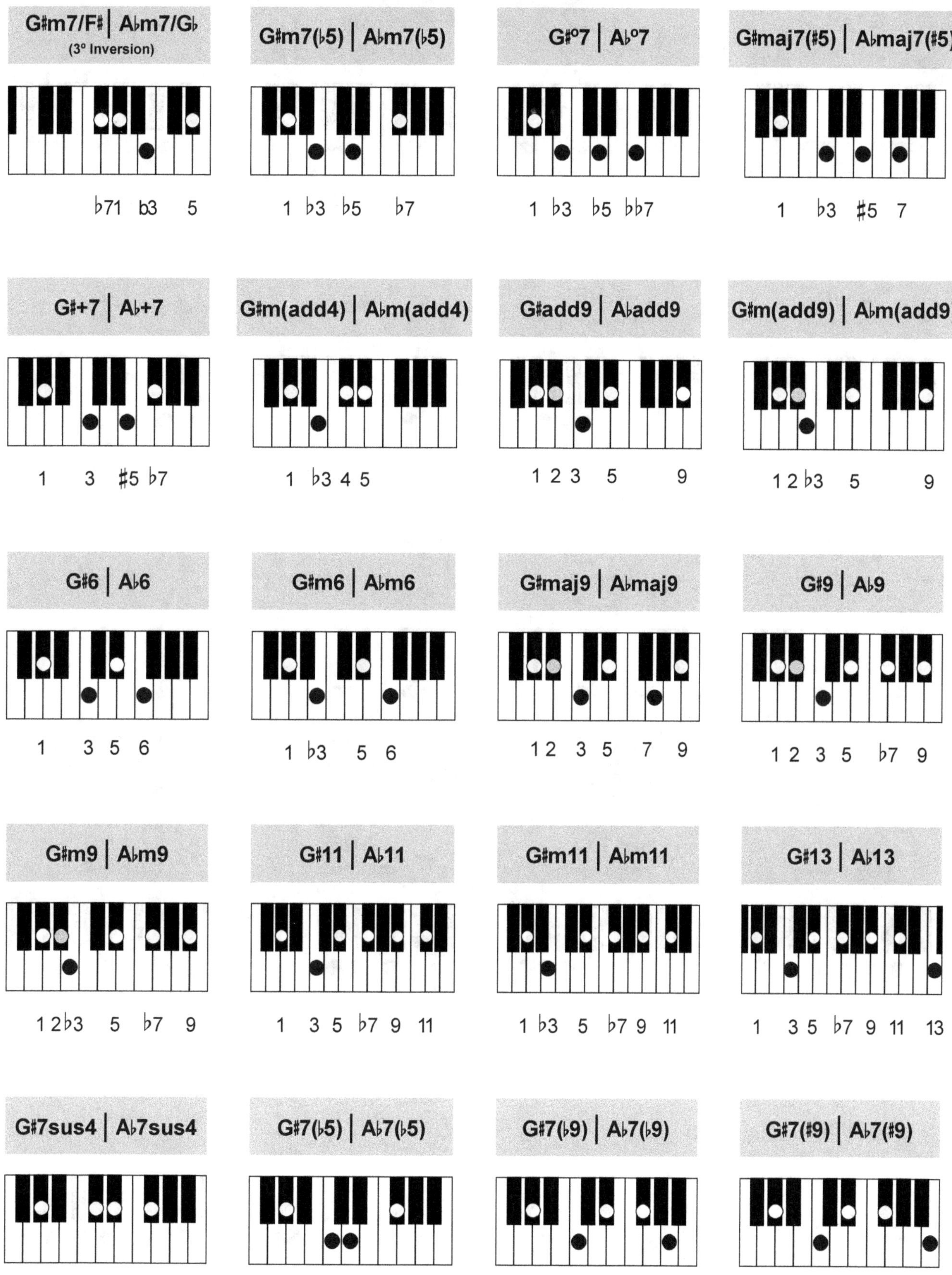

A

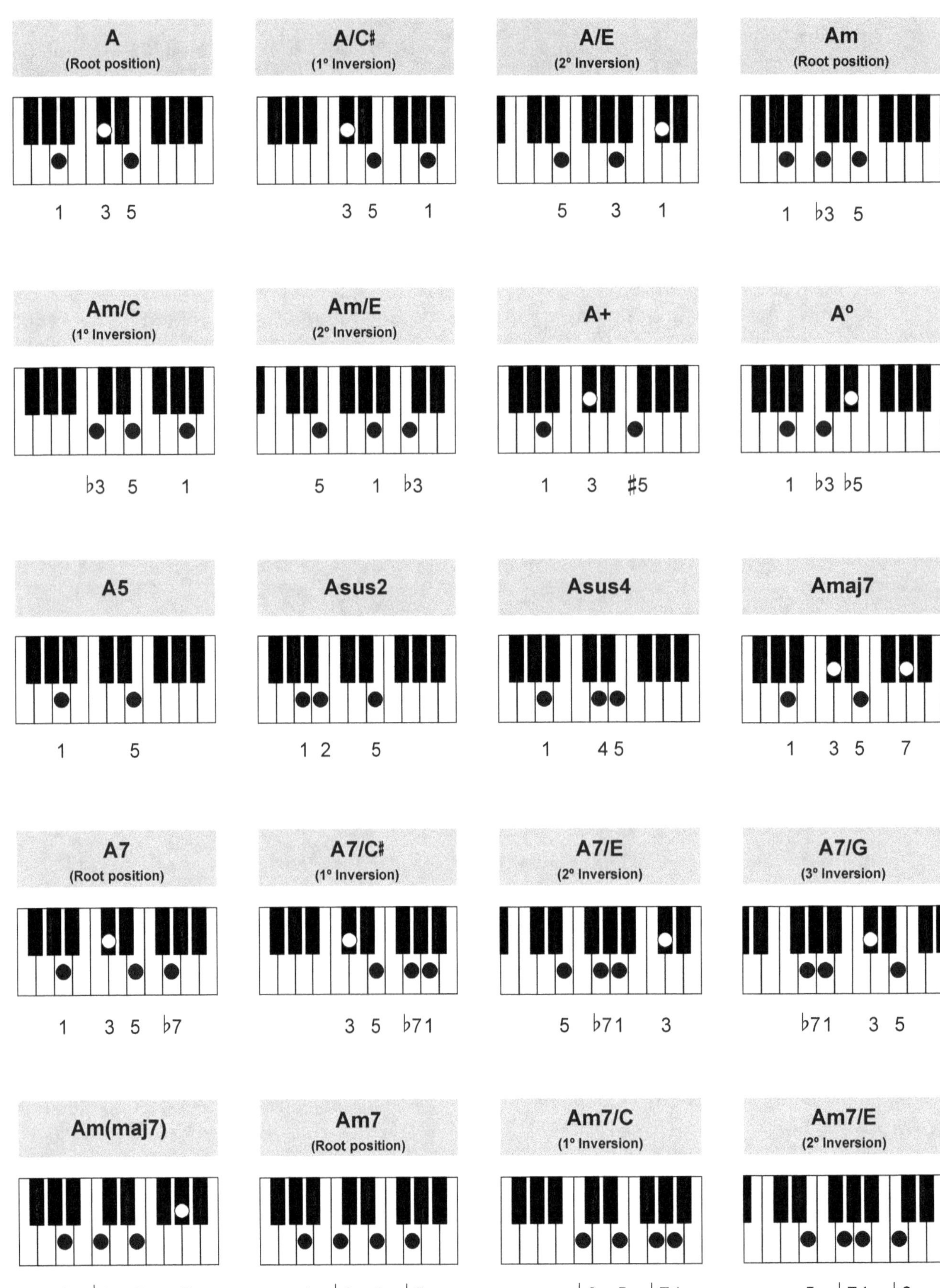

A (Root position) — 1 3 5

A/C♯ (1° Inversion) — 3 5 1

A/E (2° Inversion) — 5 3 1

Am (Root position) — 1 ♭3 5

Am/C (1° Inversion) — ♭3 5 1

Am/E (2° Inversion) — 5 1 ♭3

A+ — 1 3 ♯5

A° — 1 ♭3 ♭5

A5 — 1 5

Asus2 — 1 2 5

Asus4 — 1 4 5

Amaj7 — 1 3 5 7

A7 (Root position) — 1 3 5 ♭7

A7/C♯ (1° Inversion) — 3 5 ♭7 1

A7/E (2° Inversion) — 5 ♭7 1 3

A7/G (3° Inversion) — ♭7 1 3 5

Am(maj7) — 1 ♭3 5 7

Am7 (Root position) — 1 ♭3 5 ♭7

Am7/C (1° Inversion) — ♭3 5 ♭7 1

Am7/E (2° Inversion) — 5 ♭7 1 ♭3

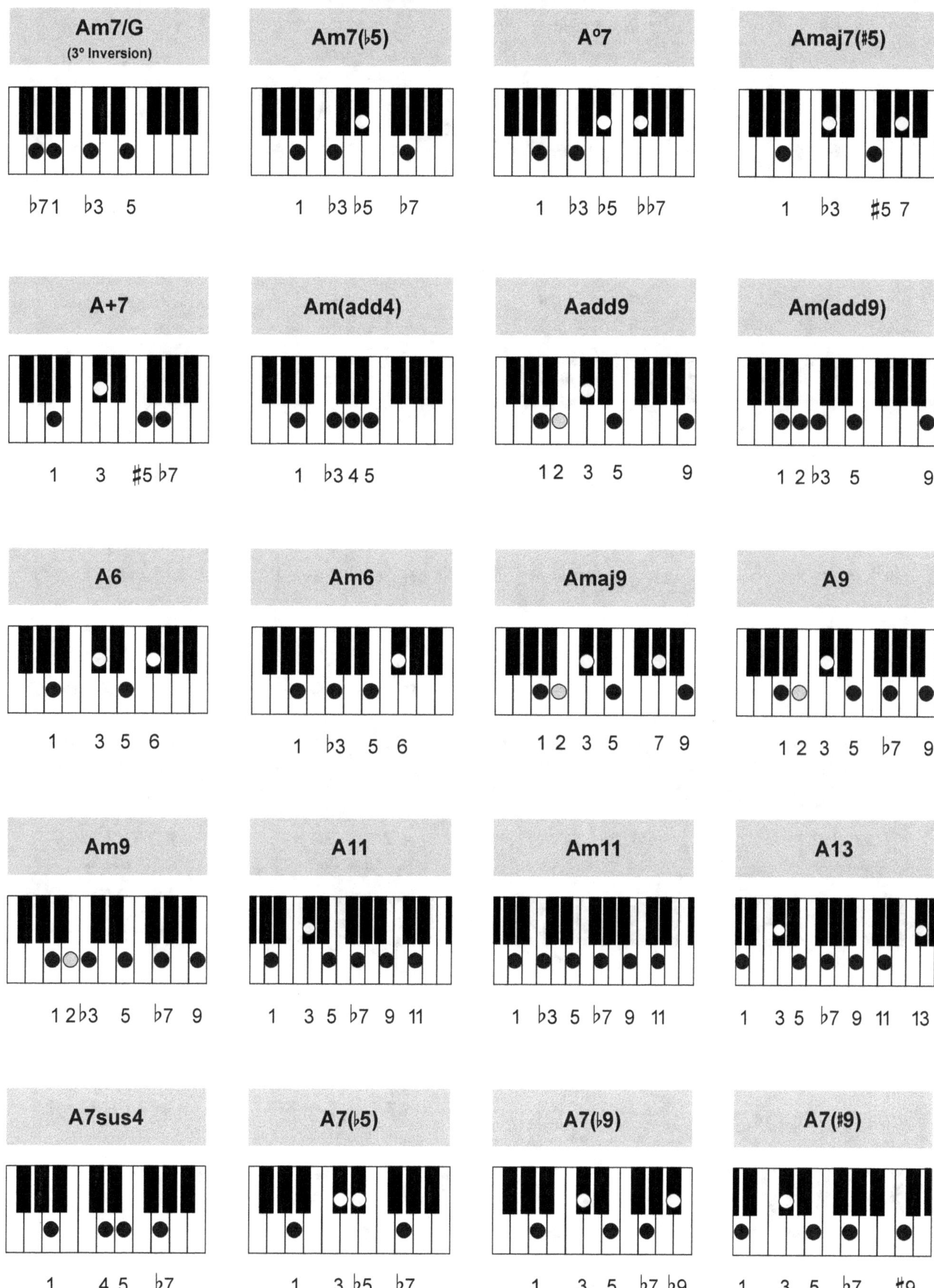

Am7/G
(3° Inversion)
♭7 1   ♭3   5

Am7(♭5)
1   ♭3 ♭5   ♭7

A°7
1   ♭3 ♭5   ♭♭7

Amaj7(♯5)
1   ♭3   ♯5 7

A+7
1   3   ♯5 ♭7

Am(add4)
1   ♭3 4 5

Aadd9
1 2   3   5   9

Am(add9)
1 2 ♭3   5   9

A6
1   3 5 6

Am6
1   ♭3   5   6

Amaj9
1 2   3   5   7 9

A9
1 2   3   5   ♭7 9

Am9
1 2 ♭3   5   ♭7   9

A11
1   3 5 ♭7 9 11

Am11
1   ♭3 5 ♭7 9 11

A13
1   3 5 ♭7 9 11 13

A7sus4
1   4 5   ♭7

A7(♭5)
1   3 ♭5   ♭7

A7(♭9)
1   3 5   ♭7 ♭9

A7(♯9)
1   3 5   ♭7   ♯9

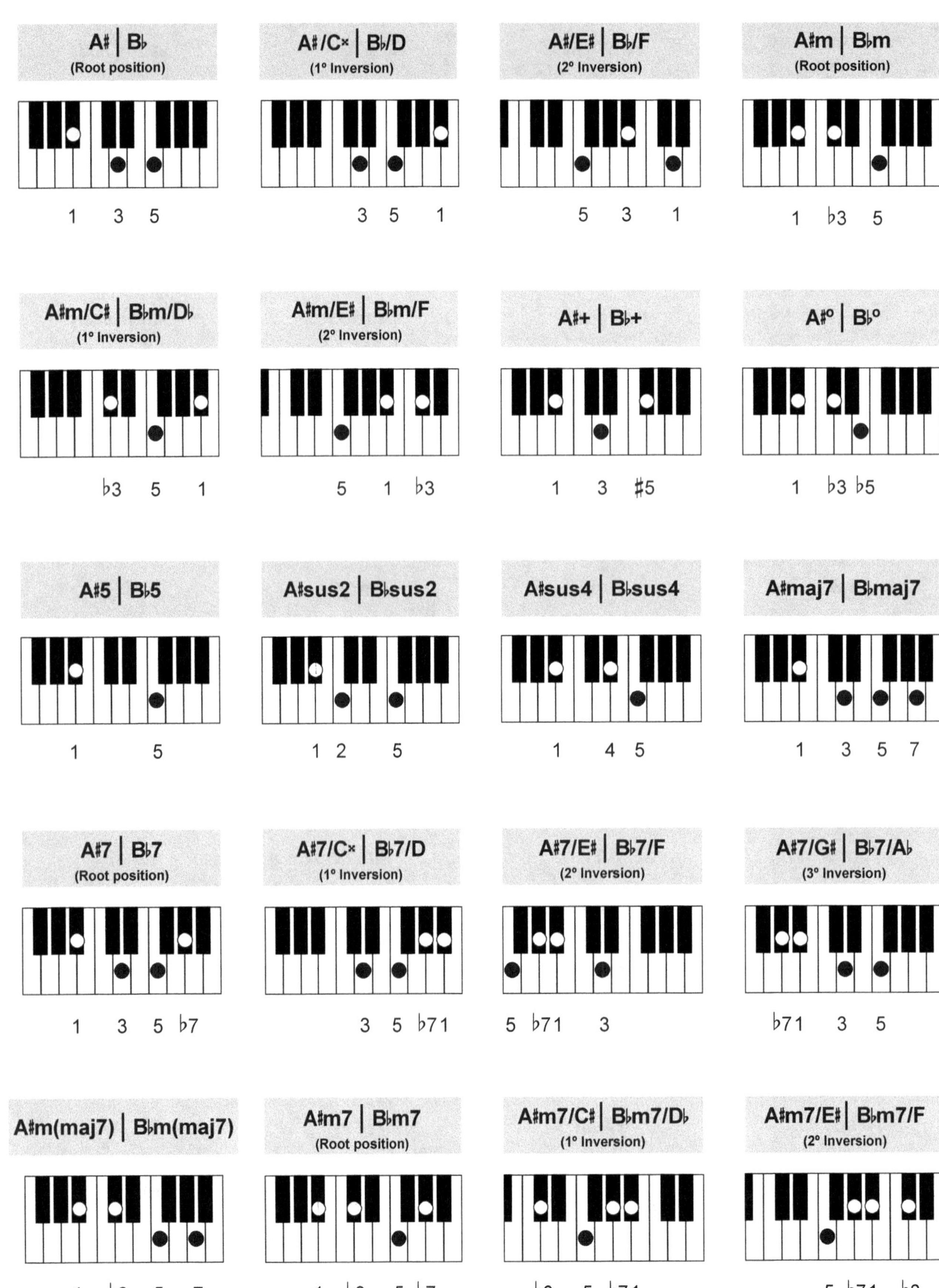

A♯ | B♭
(Root position)
1 3 5

A♯/C× | B♭/D
(1° Inversion)
3 5 1

A♯/E♯ | B♭/F
(2° Inversion)
5 3 1

A♯m | B♭m
(Root position)
1 ♭3 5

A♯m/C♯ | B♭m/D♭
(1° Inversion)
♭3 5 1

A♯m/E♯ | B♭m/F
(2° Inversion)
5 1 ♭3

A♯+ | B♭+
1 3 ♯5

A♯° | B♭°
1 ♭3 ♭5

A♯5 | B♭5
1 5

A♯sus2 | B♭sus2
1 2 5

A♯sus4 | B♭sus4
1 4 5

A♯maj7 | B♭maj7
1 3 5 7

A♯7 | B♭7
(Root position)
1 3 5 ♭7

A♯7/C× | B♭7/D
(1° Inversion)
3 5 ♭7 1

A♯7/E♯ | B♭7/F
(2° Inversion)
5 ♭7 1 3

A♯7/G♯ | B♭7/A♭
(3° Inversion)
♭7 1 3 5

A♯m(maj7) | B♭m(maj7)
1 ♭3 5 7

A♯m7 | B♭m7
(Root position)
1 ♭3 5 ♭7

A♯m7/C♯ | B♭m7/D♭
(1° Inversion)
♭3 5 ♭7 1

A♯m7/E♯ | B♭m7/F
(2° Inversion)
5 ♭7 1 ♭3

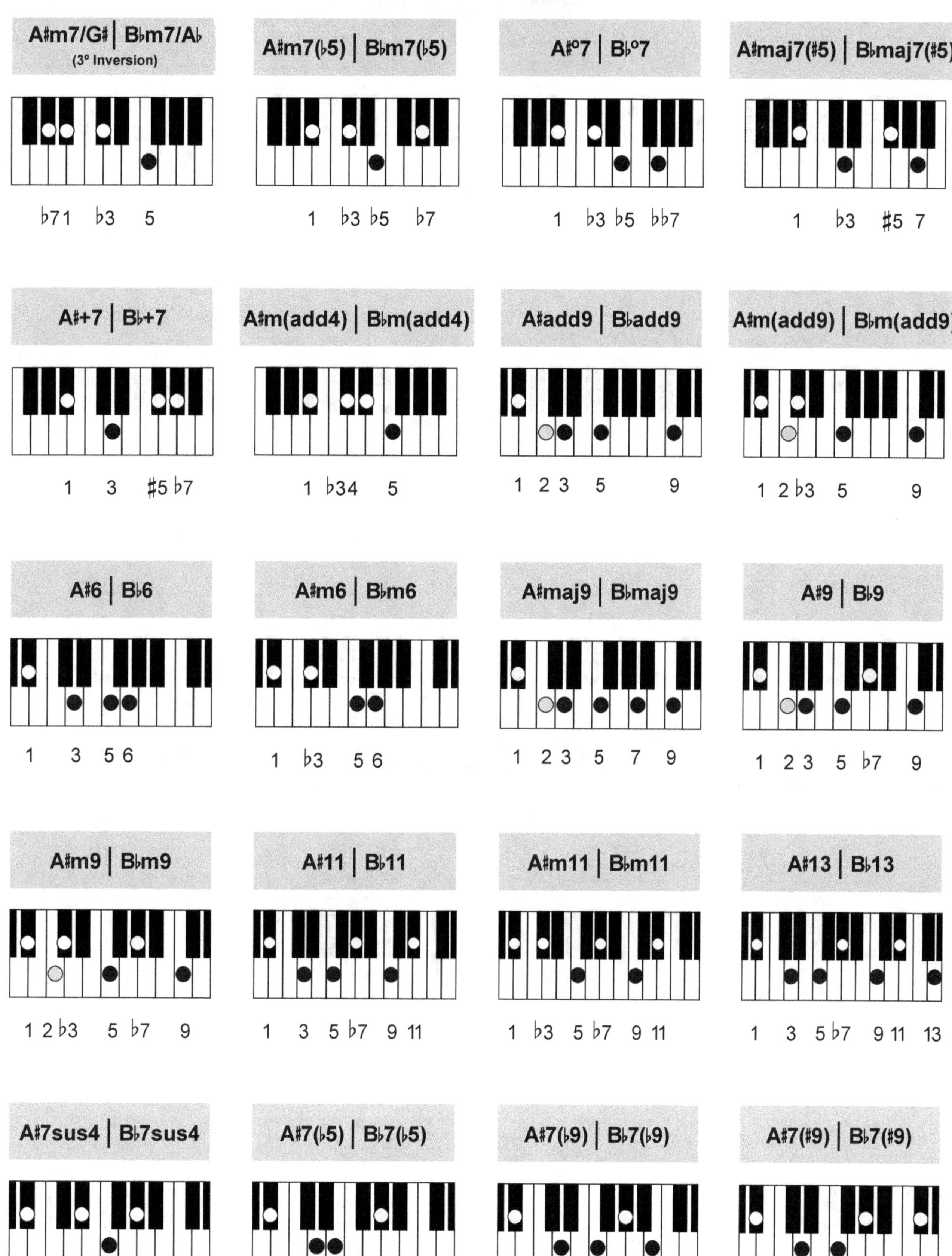

A# | Bb

A#m7/G# | Bbm7/Ab
(3º Inversion)
b7 1 b3 5

A#m7(b5) | Bbm7(b5)
1 b3 b5 b7

A#º7 | Bbº7
1 b3 b5 bb7

A#maj7(#5) | Bbmaj7(#5)
1 b3 #5 7

A#+7 | Bb+7
1 3 #5 b7

A#m(add4) | Bbm(add4)
1 b3 4 5

A#add9 | Bbadd9
1 2 3 5 9

A#m(add9) | Bbm(add9)
1 2 b3 5 9

A#6 | Bb6
1 3 5 6

A#m6 | Bbm6
1 b3 5 6

A#maj9 | Bbmaj9
1 2 3 5 7 9

A#9 | Bb9
1 2 3 5 b7 9

A#m9 | Bbm9
1 2 b3 5 b7 9

A#11 | Bb11
1 3 5 b7 9 11

A#m11 | Bbm11
1 b3 5 b7 9 11

A#13 | Bb13
1 3 5 b7 9 11 13

A#7sus4 | Bb7sus4
1 4 5 b7

A#7(b5) | Bb7(b5)
1 3 b5 b7

A#7(b9) | Bb7(b9)
1 3 5 b7 b9

A#7(#9) | Bb7(#9)
1 3 5 b7 #9

B

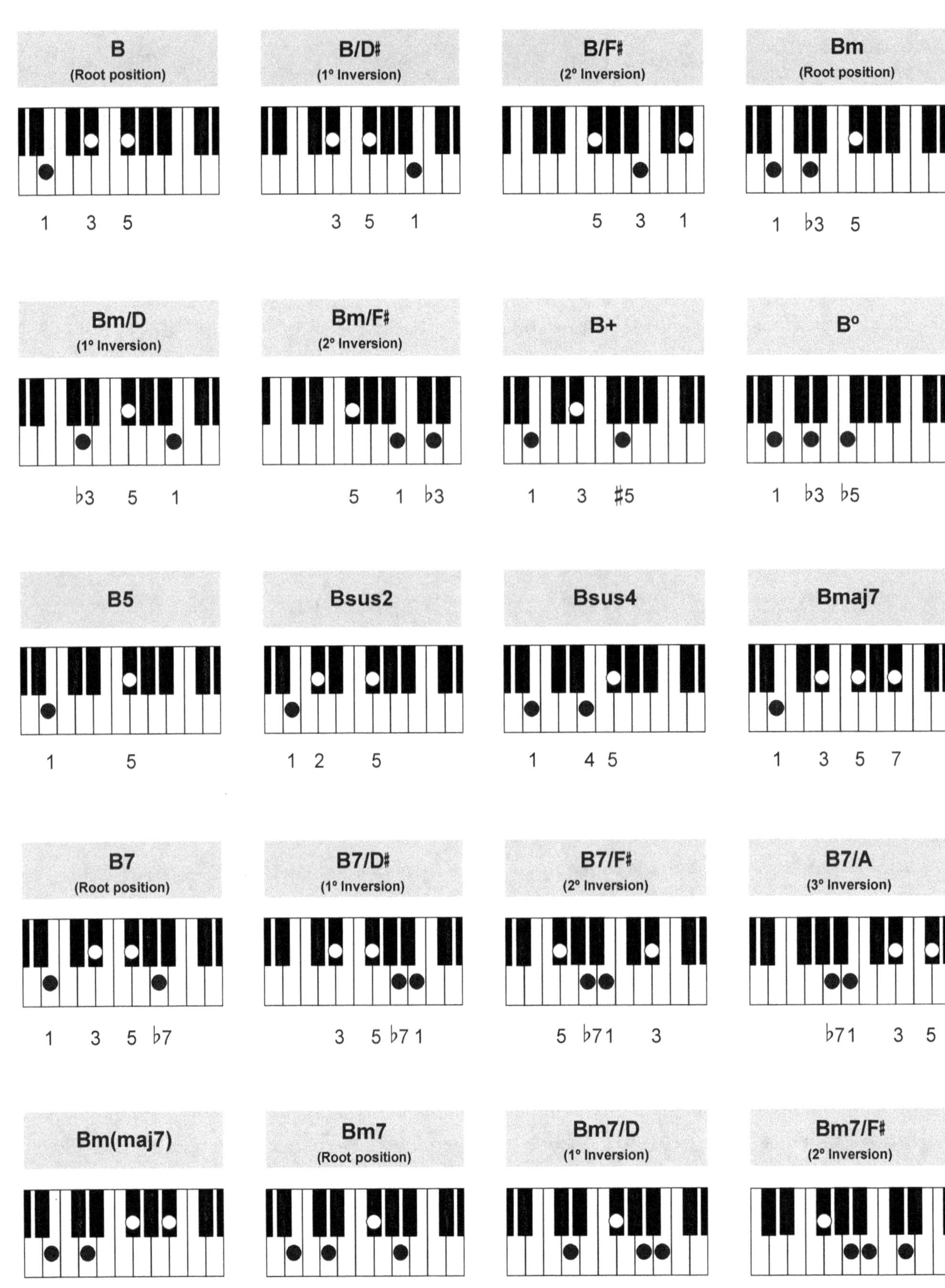

B

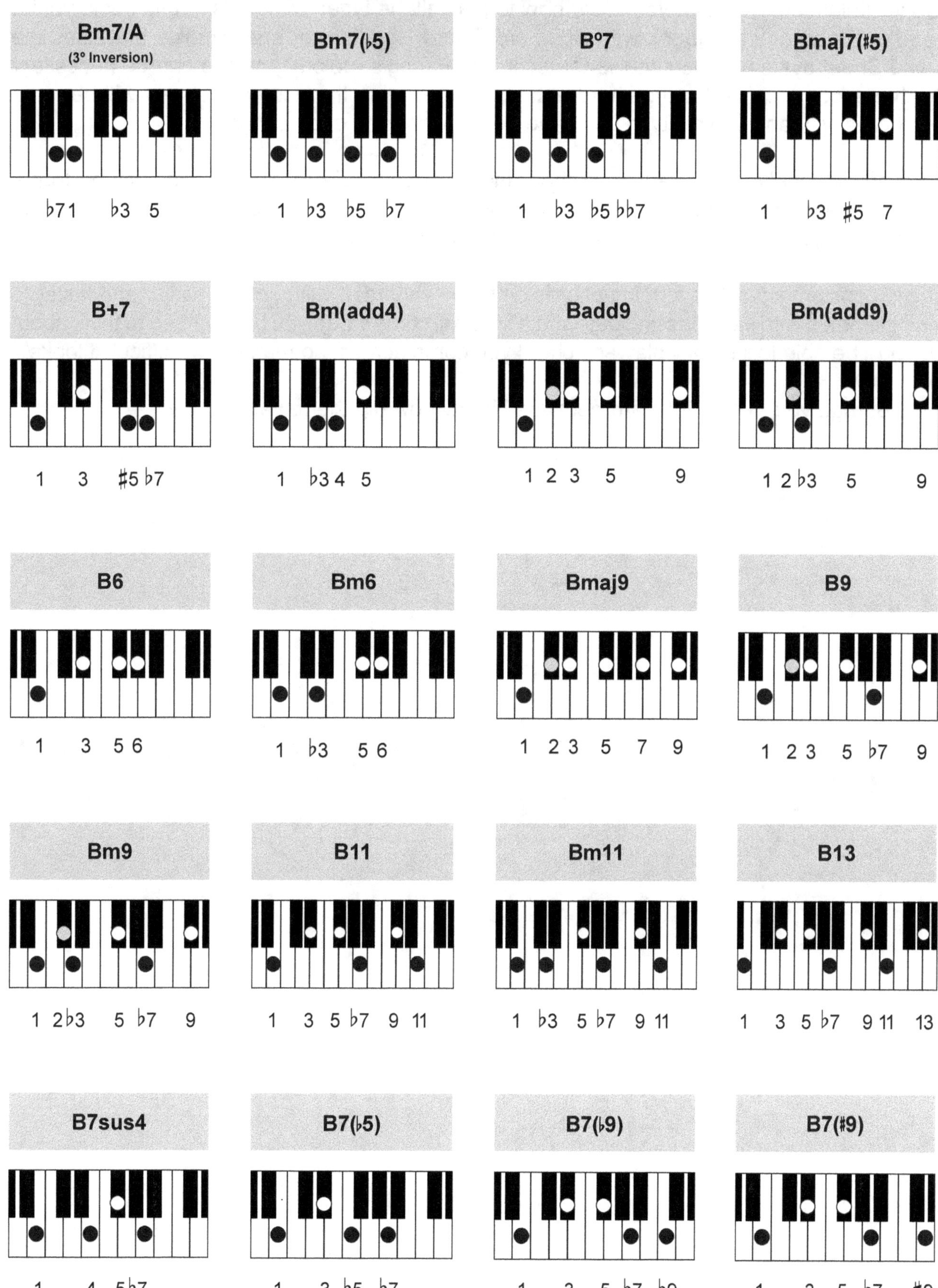

FINAL WORDS

Congratulations! Now that you know how to play all the types of chords in this book, you're ready to read any songbook with Standard Chord Notation, or sheet music that uses the Lead Sheet system, which shows the score of a song's melody and the chords necessary for the accompaniment using chord notation. Developing the accompaniment will be up to your creativity and originality in using the notes offered by each chord.

In this book, we've analyzed each chord independently. The next challenge will be to put this knowledge into action. To do that, I recommend you look up the chords to your favorite songs and go through the exercise of forming them as they appear.

If you constantly practice forming chords on the keyboard, it will become easier and faster to find the notes with each passing day, and a time will come when you barely need to think about it. You'll be able to instantly play any chord you come across, no matter how difficult it looks.

I encourage you to practice hard because I know how big the reward will be.